Tragedy, Murder & Mayhem

Bruce L. Douglass
Standish Historical Society

Edited by Lil Barcaski

Published by: GWN Publishing
www.GWNPublishing.com

Cover Design: Kristina Conatser

ISBN: 978-1-959608-95-0

This book is dedicated to the love of my life,
Cynthia Mary Reynolds Douglass,
on the occasion of our 30th anniversary.

Outrageous Case of Kidnapping

We were yesterday put in possession of the particulars of a most bold and outrageous case of kidnapping. It occurred in Steep Falls, Standish, Me. The following are briefly the particulars: Last Friday noon, as the son of Dr. J. P. Weeks, a boy four years old was going to school, a horse and chaise passed through the village, and just as it reached the place where were several children, two women got out, seized Dr. Weeks' boy, and taking him into the chaise, drove off. Dr. W. did not hear of the circumstance till nearly dark, when he went in pursuit of the kidnappers. It appeared that the women drove to Gorham, 15 miles, where they took the cars to Portland. At Portland, they look the steamer St. Lawrence, and arrived in this city Saturday morning. At 8 o'clock they took cars for Springfield. From thence they proceeded to Dalton, a village near New York line. From this place they traveled six miles on foot, and in the night, the boy in the meantime suffering extreme physical agony.

Dr. Weeks continued to follow them, and on Monday, in company with Sheriff Tuttle, of Hendills, found the kidnappers with the kidnapped boy, in a house two miles from any neighbors, in a wild and mountainous region. The women refused to surrender the boy, and resisted the officer most pertinaciously. In fact, they fought like desperadoes, and in the encounter Sheriff Tuttle was personally much injured. The clothes of the women were nearly, torn from their bodies in the melee. They were finally taken into custody, and conveyed to the county jail, where they will remain till a requisition for their surrender is forwarded from the Governor of Maine to the Governor of New York.

Dr. Weeks returned to the city yesterday, and last evening proceeded homewards, delighted, of course, to obtain his boy, who is a bright and handsome little fellow.

The kidnappers carried their charge over six hundred miles. One of the women is about fifty years old, and the other about twenty-five. The six miles they traveled on foot was over a range of the Green Mountains. Their names are suppressed at the request of Dr. Weeks. It is enough that they are secured, and that justice will be dealt out to them for their high crime.

The mother of the child was nearly insane from her loss; which ere this has been changed to joy. This is one of the boldest and most novel cases of kidnapping that has occurred of late years. [Boston Bee.]

— **Maine Farmer, July 21, 1852**

Melancholy Accident

On the 22d inst. Messrs. Edmund Fowler, Lesting Laflin, and Matthew McCulley of Gorham, and William Orr, of Standish, with his son aged about 10 years, were on Sebago Pond on a fishing party. On their return, towards sunset, as is supposed, the boat was capsized in a sudden squall of wind and they were all drowned. Their hats have since been found on Indian Island. Messrs., Fowlers and Laflin were of the firm of Edmund Fowler &. Co. of the Cumberland Powder Manufactory, in Gorham, and Mr. McCulley, a native of Ireland, and a single man, was foreman of that establishment. The two former gentlemen were natives of Southwick, Mass. Mr. Fowler has left a family in said town, and Mr. Laflin was recently married. Mr. Orr has also left a wife and family.—Eastern Argus

— **American Advocate, June 30, 1827**

Steep Falls

William C. Fogg, a heading maker at T. & J. H. Lord's mill, while lugging in boards last Friday in jumping out of the way of a pile of boards that was tipping over, jumped so far that he went off from the wharf, falling a distance of 25 feet to the bottom of the river. The water was four or five feet deep and he went under out of sight. He came up and swam to the shore, strange to say, escaping with only a slightly sprained ankle.

— Portland Daily Press, March 21, 1890

The Accident at Sebago

No particulars in regard to the accident at Standish on the line of the Portland and Ogdensburg railroad have been received that are of an official character further than that the accident occurred at a spot about four miles from Standish village at a place where there is a cut through the sand some sixty feet deep with a sloping grade. It is thought that the rain had affected the heavy bank of sand causing a slide by which six men were covered. One of the men, it is reported, although the report lacks confirmation, died yesterday morning, whose name was Smith, and another named Kearney, so seriously injured that he was not expected to survive. The other four were not very badly hurt. One of the engineers has gone out to the spot and will probably return this noon when we shall get the particulars

— **Portland Daily Press, May 12, 1870**

Workers Buried

The Argus says that six of the laborers at work in the cut at Standish, section 15 of the Portland and Ogdensburg railroad, were buried, or partly so, by the falling in of the bank on Tuesday. It is reported that two of those injured have since died.

— Bath Daily Times, May 13, 1870

Arrested on Serious Charge

Steep Falls Man Brought Here To Face Accusation of Assault

Michael Sarara, employed on the new dam at Steep Falls, was arrested this morning by Deputy Sheriff Charles R. Murch of Baldwin, on a charge of assault with serious intent on Mrs. Odette, wife of Napoleon Odette, a wood chopper, who lives in a little shack about a mile from Steep Falls. Sarara went to the shack yesterday and threw Odette out and locked the door. Mrs. Odette was in the shack with her four children. Sarara attempted to assault her but the woman's husband broke in the door before the woman was injured. Sarara as he left the shack was followed for some distance by Odette but as Sarara threatened him with a revolver he gave up the chase. This morning he was arrested by Deputy Murch at the store at Steep Falls and brought to this City. He was intoxicated at the time of the attempted assault.

— Portland Daily Press, December 27, 1905

Waterworks Accident

Last Thursday a man named William Smith, employed on the water works at Lake Sebago, in Standish, was accidentally hit on the head with a sledge hammer, which fell a distance of 22 feet, crushing his skull in such a manner that he cannot possibly recover. He is about 40 years of age, and leaves a wife and six children in England.

— **Portland Daily Press, December 27, 1869**

Shocking Accident

An explosion took place in one of the Powder Mills in Gorham, July 19th which occasioned the death of six of the workmen, viz:—Wm. Moses, Noah Babb and James Green, of Standish—Josiah Clark, Jr. and Hanson Irish, of Gorham, and! Major Means, of Windham—all young men without families. Daniel Moses, of Standish, was also injured to such a degree that his life was despaired of, although he was alive on Monday morning. The melancholy accident, says the Portland Advertiser of yesterday, was occasioned in exchanging the composition from one mortar to another. A young man, unacquainted with the work, to loosen some of it from the mortar, dropped the copper pestle. He was told to desist by one of the workmen, but repeated it three times, when the powder took fire and exploded about sixteen casks.

— **American Advocate, July 25, 1828**

Over 300 Pigs Burned In Standish Piggery

Between 300 and 400 pigs were burned yesterday in a piggery at Standish. owned by Herbert L. Berry of this city. A small camp nearby also was burned. The loss on the pigs was estimated at $1000

— Daily Kennebec Journal, March 3, 1926

Fire

A fire was discovered in the Powder Keg manufactory of John Lindsey, in Standish, at the head of the Cumberland and Oxford canal on Monday night at about half past 9 o'clock. Two buildings were totally consumed. Loss estimated at about $4000, partially insured at the agency of W. D. Little. By this disaster about thirty-five men are thrown out of employment.

— **Bangor Daily Journal, October 27, 1859**

Mill Destroyed

Fire in Standish, Maine —On Saturday last, the buildings known as the "Bonny Eagle Mills were destroyed. There were two buildings; containing 4 saws and a box machine. The value was about $2000— total loss.

— Commercial Advertiser, November 6, 1847

York's Corner Fire

The Argus says that the store of Mr. Edwin Norton at York's Corner, Standish, was totally destroyed by fire Friday. A new and quite large stock of goods had recently been put into the store, which was also burned. The fire was occasioned by a defective chimney.

— Maine Farmer, June 10, 1876

Highway Robbery

A Mr. Alfred Foss, of Standish, was returning home from Portland on Thursday last, where he had collected $300, and when within two miles of Limerick village was attacked by two men who sprang into the road, dragged him from the sleigh, beat him insensible, and then robbed him. A pistol ball was discharged through his clothing. Foss was soon after discovered by his neighbors and cared for. The Portland police have arrested two young men on suspicion of having committed the deed.

— **Bangor Daily Evening Times, February 18, 1867**

Fire at Standish Village

Yesterday morning at about two o'clock, the dwelling house owned by Marshall S. and Albion P. Howe was discovered to be on fire. At the time of the discovery, the fire had made such progress as to render it impossible to extinguish it. The house, sheds and stable were consumed. A portion of the furniture was saved. The house has been unoccupied for several weeks, and it is highly probable that this fire was the work of an incendiary.

— **Daily Eastern Argus, June 28, 1866**

A Horrible Thing

**An Aged Lady at Standish Found Dead in Bed,
With Features Terribly Disfigured,
It is Supposed, by Cats,
After Having Died from Natural Causes
During Wednesday Night.**

Portland, March 7.—A horrible story comes from Standish, this morning. Only the most meager details can be learned in regard to it, but there is said to be little question of its truth. An old lady named Mrs. Pease, who lived with a man named Skillings, in the western part of the town of Standish, went to bed, last night, in her usual good health. She was about 70 years old and had hardly suffered a sick day in her life. This morning, when her bedroom door was opened, she was found dead in bed. It is said that her nose and ears were eaten almost off, and her face was disfigured by the scratches and claws of some animal supposed to be a cat, of which there were several about the house. It is supposed the woman died from natural causes, and after her death her face was thus horribly mangled.

— Daily Kennebec Journal, March 8, 1895

Into a Deep Hole

Two Standish Lads Go Wading and Both Are Drowned.

Standish. Me. May 22.—The warm wave yesterday was responsible In part for the death of two Standish boys, who late in the afternoon removed their shoes and stockings and waded into Jose's brook. They walked into a deep hole and were drowned. The victims were James B. 13, son of Franklin Norton, and Walter E. 11, son of Edgar S. Norton. The fathers are cousins and the latter is proprietor of a local hotel. Carl Boulter, aged 8. was the only witness of the accident. He screamed lustily for help and within two or three minutes assistance was at hand, but the bodies were not recovered for an hour.

— **Daily Kennebec Journal, May 23, 1911**

Mast Tree Death

On the 30th ult. George Cummings, the only, and very promising son of Mr. Thomas Cummings, of Standish, (Maine) was in instantly killed by being caught under a roller upon which a mast tree was then drawing.

— Pittsfield Sun, October 24, 1803

Breaking & Entering

Thomas Dunsier, breaking and entering the dwelling house of Betsey O. Wilson, pleaded guilty. Stated his age 17; that one Bragdon got him drunk and suggested the idea of going into the house; don't know what became of the money they took; never was before Court before; mother dead; father living. The County Attorney nol prossed the allegation as to the night time. Sentenced to six months in the county jail.

John Bragdon, breaking and entering dwelling house of Betsey O. Wilson. Pleaded guilty. Stated his age as 19; father and mother lives in Standish: was out to Saccarappa looking for work, got drunk and broke into the house; been before the Court once before on a charge of breaking and entering; been in the army, got homesick and deserted. Sentenced to three years in state prison.

— **Portland Daily Press, May 10, 1870**

Infant Drowned

An infant son of Chas. Kemp, of Standish. was drowned in the Cumberland and Oxford canal, on the 28th ult. He dropped a toy in the canal, and reaching down to get it, fell into the water. The body was recovered.

— Christian Mirror, August 5, 1876

Over the Dam

Narrow Escape of N. H. Sawyer at Bonny Eagle.
Saved from the Icy Jaws of Death Just In Time
Pulled Out on the End of a Rope.

Mr. E. G. Carl, of Buxton Center, was in the city yesterday and reported the following remarkable experience of N. H. Sawyer of Bonny Eagle in which he had a narrow escape from a terrible death.

Tuesday, Mr. Sawyer was at work on the river just above the dam at the Came saw mills at Bonny Eagle. For a short distance above the dam there was clear water and of course very swift current The dam is some fifteen feet high, and the river flowing over it makes a fierce and furious waterfall. Just below the falls there is a space of open water and very swift current which flows rapidly under the ice.

Mr. Sawyer was at work above the dam clearing away the ice from the logs. He slipped and fell into the water and was carried over the dam.

Very fortunately another man saw the whole thing. With great presence of mind he seized a coil of rope and rushed down below the dam. There was only one place where he could get across to the open water. He reached that in time and threw the rope to Mr. Sawyer as he was swept past by the swift current. The distance was short. Sawyer seized the rope and was pulled ashore none the worse for the experience except for the wetting and the chill of the icy water.

As he himself said, if he hadn't been seen just in time and rescued just so promptly be would surely have been swept under the ice, the edge of which was, of course, sharp and thin around that open space of swift water.

To have seized the ice as he was swept down upon it and drawn himself out of the swift current would have been well-nigh an impossibility, even if a man hadn't just received the unnerving shock of being carried over a waterfall in the middle of winter.

— **Portland Daily Press, January 16, 1896**

Indecent Assault

SUPEME JUDICIAL COURT.
CRIMINAL TERM—WALTON, J. PRESIDING.
Monday—The Court came in at 3 P. M.

Amos Goodale was put upon trial on charge of indecent assault upon a Mrs. Shaw of Standish. The prisoner is a man 73 years of age, and Mrs. S. a comely lady well past the heyday of youth. The prisoner is a pedlar, and the assault is alleged to have been made in complainant's house, in the absence of her husband. Verdict guilty.

— Daily Eastern Argus, August 14, 1866

Deadly Accident at Reservoir

Standish, May 13.—-C. J. Ingalls died at his residence in this place, aged 33 years, the result of an accident received one week ago.

Mr. Ingalls and another young man rode over to the reservoir being built by the Portland Water Company. Their horse suddenly turned and threw them out. Mr. Ingalls struck on a sharp rock, breaking his wrist and cutting it badly. Erysipelas set in and death resulted after intense suffering for one week.

The funeral was held Tuesday from union chapel. Rev. Alonzo Stevens of South Windham officiated, assisted by Rev. G. K. Goodwin of Standish. The Brother Knights attended in a body, performing the last rites at the grave. The floral offerings were choice and beautiful.

Mr. Ingalls leaves a wife and three small children, besides a father, mother and three brothers.

— Portland Daily Press, May 14, 1903

Fire in Standish

The dwelling house of Mr. Thorn, on Oakhill, Standish, was destroyed by fire about 1 o'clock, last Monday morning. It is presumed that it was the work of an incendiary.

— Portland Daily Press, July 23, 1866

Break-in and Theft

A term of the S. J. Court commenced in this town on Tuesday last. The Grand Jury found but two indictments, one against Richard Rosse for breaking into a store and stealing goods from it in Standish, and the other against Charles B. Mason, for carrying off a horse and chaise belonging to Messrs. Noyes & Fobes of this town, with intent to keep it. Both pleaded guilty, and the first was sentenced to four years hard labor in the State Prison. The sentence of the latter was suspended until the fall term of the Court, from some peculiar circumstances which his situation presented.

— **Eastern Argus, May 7, 1830**

Sudden Death

Mr. Joseph Martin, of Naples, last Thursday paid a visit to his daughter in Standish. On returning home in company with a daughter, he got out of the sleigh to walk up a hill. Before reaching the brow of the hill he complained of his head, and got into the sleigh. In a few moments, he pitched forward and expired. He was about 58 years of age.

— **Portland Daily Press, January 17, 1866**

Accidental Discharge

In Standish, Wednesday night, about three miles above Sebago lake there was a tragedy which resulted in the death of James Adams, a laborer living in the town. The affair took place at the house of one Kraery, who lives alone in a neighborhood that is not thickly settled. At the house were Emery Adams and a man named Elwell, who belongs in Buxton and has been at work during the winter in Standish. The men had a shot gun and were handling it looking at it or something of the kind. In some way the gun was discharged and the charge of shot struck Adams full in the head, killing him instantly.

— **Somerset Reporter, January 25, 1900**

Hotel Destroyed by Fire

The Portland Argus says that Wednesday, the hotel at Steep Falls, Standish, with all the out-buildings, including a fine large stable, were completely destroyed by fire. The property was owned by Col. Luke Rich, and occupied by Messrs. Norton & Kennison. The fire originated in the attic of the hotel, probably through a defect in the chimney.

— Christian Mirror, August 5, 1876

Town Papers Destroyed

**Burglars Do Irreparable Damage to
Contents of Safe at Standish.**

Portland, Me., May 1. — Town of Standish notes, deeds and papers valued at several hundred dollars, according to a special to the Express, were destroyed early Tuesday by burglars who, in blowing open the safe in the Standish post office, used an overcharge of explosive.

The papers were torn to pieces and the post office was partially wrecked. Stamps to the value of $118 and $2 in cash were secured and the burglars escaped, A post office inspector in this city was notified and left on the morning train to investigate.

— Daily Kennebec Journal, May, 2, 1906

Larceny Charge

The Portland Star says that in the Portland Municipal Court, Wednesday, Sarah Kemp, of Standish, was before the court, charged with larceny. The complainant was Mr. Jeremiah Parker, of Gorham. The case was continued four weeks. It is said that a partial confession and worse things to come was the occasion of the continuance. Respondent held in two hundred dollars bail. It is believed that she was only acting an unimportant part in a very large affair.

— **Lewiston Evening Journal, January 17, 1868**

Melancholy Circumstance

Wednesday the 17th inst., a Mr. Tarbox and his wife who resided on a gore of land between the towns of Raymond and Standish were frozen to death.

It appears that their family consisted of four small children, the youngest at the breast; being in very necessitous circumstances, Mr. Tarbox started on Wednesday, during the violence of the gale and drifting snow, to procure some aid from the neighbors, about five miles distant. Having obtained a supply for their immediate wants, he placed it in a bag and proceeded for home. It seems, however, that, when within about one mile of his house, the weight of his load compelled him to leave it upon a tree and endeavor to reach his distressed family without it—but his efforts were in this also frustrated, overpowered with fatigue, he stopped about 80 rods from home and cried for help, his wife hearing the voice went to his assistance, and as is presumed, from the circumstance of hiding her cloak and handkerchief upon the man, her pressing wants induced her to leave him and hasten to procure the provisions. But alas! her strength did not equal her resolution—she expired in the effort, and her body was found but a short distance from the provisions her partner had placed upon the tree.

On the day following, the eldest child went out and found her father's corpse, and returned to the house and commenced sounding a horn, used for calling distant workmen to their meals; this, however, brought no one to their assistance through the day—but the continuance of the sound on the succeeding day led a number to the spot to witness this shocking affair, and to the relief of a family who had remained three days without sustenance.

— Centinel of Freedom, April 20, 1819

Burglary

Burglary. Friday night the store of Mr. Clough at Standish lower corner, was broken into and a lot of boots, flannel, shirts, hair oil, etc., was taken. Among other articles was an old lot of counterfeit bills on the State banks which Mr. Clough had kept for years in the back part of his safe. The safe was broken into. It was evidently the work of experts and probably the same gang who broke into the store of Hanson the night before.

— Maine Farmer, November 1, 1873

Murder in Standish

Killing of John McCarthy by William Logan

Testimony at the Coroner's Inquest.

The following is descriptive of an appalling crime to be added to the long list of those instigated by the intoxicating cup, and should prove a lesson so needed by those who have taken steps down the ladder leading to crime, the drunkard's grave, and perdition.

The circumstances in this case are as follows, and we take the reader through the primary steps ending in the killing of John McCarthy by William Logan.

The parties were in the employ of Messrs. Hugh Dolan and Shannihan, sub-contractors on the Portland and Ogdensburg Railroad, and with the rest of the employees were paid off on Thursday. With their money and in company with two other men, Thursday night, they bought liquors and enjoyed their debauch at the house of Logan. Tired with each other's company, and stupefied with liquor, they disposed of themselves for the night, Logan with his wife retiring to their bedroom leading by a door, without a fastening, to the sitting room. One of the party, a man named James J. Berrigan, while under the influence of what he had been taking, became very sociable, and going into the bed-room where Logan and his wife were in bed, he made indecent overtures to the woman. She told her husband what Berrigan was doing, and which so maddened the husband that he jumped out of bed and pitched into Berrigan giving him a couple of black eyes and beating him till he cried enough.— Berrigan left the house and Logan retired. McCarthy, who was present at the battle, said to Logan that he did just right, and if any man had attempted the same on a wife of his, he would serve him the same. McCarthy stopped there all night and took in breakfast and dinner on Friday, with sundry potations from the black bottle, replenished in a shanty nearby. One other of their boon companions was entertained in the same manner.

Now we come to the scene of the murder, and we take the facts from the testimony of a coroner's inquest, which was held after the death of McCarthy, Coroner Hall, of this city, presiding.

Mrs. Sarah Malinda Logan, wife of the man charged with the murder, testified that she had known McCarthy about two weeks; that he had often been at the house; that about 2 o'clock on Friday, Logan (her husband) and McCarthy commenced sparring; that they got mad with each other; Logan clinched McCarthy in the house, knocked him down, did not strike him, but dragged him out of doors; McCarthy got up and went into Burk's shanty (the place where they had purchased their liquor) and then came out with an iron used to take covers from the stove and shake down the ashes; that he struck Logan with it on the head and drew blood; Logan then took the iron away from McCarthy in the struggle that ensued and with it inflicted a blow on the latter's head and left him lying on the ground; McCarthy crawled to Burk's shanty and said, when he reached the door, "For God's sake let me in;" that both McCarthy and Logan were so drunk that they could not walk straight; they had had no previous quarrel; Logan did not order McCarthy out of the house.

Ellen Burk testified that when she came along the road, about the time named, Mrs. Logan said to her, "McCarthy is killing my husband;" saw Logan dragging McCarthy out of the house by his feet; McCarthy immediately came to her house, and asked for a stick; he took the stove cover lifter and went out; saw Logan strike McCarthy with a club of wood; McCarthy fell upon his face, and Logan ran to the road; Mrs. Logan said that "McCarthy is killed." McCarthy crawled to her door and did not stand on his feet afterwards; did not see Logan use the iron; McCarthy stayed in her house till he died, which was about half past twelve o'clock Saturday; think McCarthy was intoxicated. Logan was.

Dr. Cobb testified he was called to see McCarthy in Burk's house about half past eleven o'clock Friday night; found his breathing labored, his extremities cold, and seeming very weak and unconscious; McCarthy had a wound over his right eye, 2 1/2 inches long, extending to the skull; would not risk his opinion that the blow would cause death; did not think the symptoms manifested could be caused from a blow in the back; some of the symptoms might have been from intoxication.

Drs. Foster and Gordon of this city, and Dr. Cobb of Standish, were called to make a post mortem examination, which they performed yesterday. They found that the blow which McCarthy had received over the right eye could not have caused his death, but that the real cause was produced by a blow on the left side of the head. There the skin had not been broken, but the skull showed a fracture some four or five inches long. By the fracture an artery had been broken, and the blood had flown in upon the brain causing his death.

The coroner's jury returned a verdict of "death from blows by the hand of William Logan."

Deputies Bolton and Perry, who went out to Standish Saturday morning on hearing the news of the fight, arrived there shortly after McCarthy died and arrested Logan.— Berrigan they also arrested and brought to safe keeping for the assault on Logan's wife.

McCarthy was a small man, about 35 years of age, and nothing is known about him except that he had said he belonged near St. John. Logan is a large and powerful man, and hails from St. John, N. B.

— **Daily Eastern Argus, December 20, 1869**

Municipal Court

Judge Kingsbury Presiding

Wednesday - State vs. William Logan. Murder of John McCarthy in Standish. Plea, not guilty. Waived an examination and committed to await the action of the grand jury.

State vs. James Berrigan. Assault with intent to commit a rape upon the person of Sarah M. Logan, in Standish. Ordered to recognize to the State in the sum of $2000 for his appearance at the Supreme Court in January.

— **Portland Daily Press, December 23, 1869**

For Observation

**Standish Burglar Is Committed to
Maine Insane Hospital.**

Deputy Sheriff George T. Delano of South Portland returned home on the 10:43 P. M. train, Wednesday after bringing to the Maine Insane hospital Archie Cox of Shelburne, N. H., who was arrested by Sheriff Moulton for breaking and entering at Standish. Cox was held to the Cumberland county grand jury, an indictment found against him for breaking, entering, and larceny; and he was ordered by the court to be committed to the Maine Insane hospital in order that observation might be made as to his mental condition.

Cox is about 34 years of age and appears to be very stupid, scarcely returning intelligible answers to the questions asked him. He claims to have a wife and four children at Shelburne.

— **Daily Kennebec Journal, May 16, 1912**

Fatal Accident

On the 23th ult., Col. John L. Tucker, of Standish, came to his death in an untimely manner. He was engaged in taking down the frame of a saw mill at Steep Falls, in Standish. A portion of the frame fell upon Col. Tucker, dreadfully injuring and crushing him, and causing his death in a few hours. He was a worthy man, and has left a wife and three young children mournfully affected by his sudden death.— Argus.

— Gospel Banner, August 11, 1849

Fires Not Set

Insurance Commissioner G. Waldon Smith declared Tuesday that the recent investigations of the three fires occurring at Standish during the past three months proved that they were not the work of any incendiary.

"The special investigator secured, by the insurance department from New York in his report says that the fires were not set," continued Commissioner Smith.

"No two fires can be linked up, each of the three fires being separate and distinct occurrences. The third fire is still under additional investigation, the evidence on which will be submitted to the county attorney of Cumberland county in a few days. The first two fires were caused by indiscriminate, careless cigarette smoking.

"In thus clearing up these fires, it is hoped that the fears of the residents of Standish may be set at rest. There has been an uneasy feeling in that community that a firebug was at large, and the investigation positively disproves that there is any cause for such rumors."

— Daily Kennebec Journal, October 4, 1922

Illegal Hunting

Four Men Arraigned In Municipal Court for Illegally Killing Deer

William Tucker of Standish, Frank H. Brown, J. D. Sullivan, and G. K. Dunn, all of Portland, were arraigned before Judge H. H. Brazzell, In the Skowhegan Municipal court, last Friday afternoon, charged with the illegal killing of game last Fall. They were brought to trial thru the activity of Game Warden, William T. Pollard. It was alleged that the men in question not only shot their allotment of deer but left several carcasses in the woods.

The hearing was a lengthy one and much conflicting of testimony was evident. The Game Warden had as witnesses, Harvey Keyser of Kennebunk, William Peters of North Branch, and David Brown of Greenville. County Attorney T. A. Anderson appeared for the State and Merrill & Merrill for the defendants. All four men entered a plea of not guilty.

Harvey Keyser, otherwise known as Fitzsimmons, was the principal witness for the State. He was engaged at cutting wood for William R. Peters at the camp where the hunters stayed. He testified that the camp became short of deer meat and that Emmons and Sullivan told him where to find two hung up in the woods.

He furthermore stated that in his opinion the hunters intended to shoot all they could get, to have eight as big as possible to take home and to leave the small ones behind. This opinion was loudly refuted by all four hunters. Doubt was cast as to the veracity of the witness by counsel for defense. Keyser also said that he often went into the woods with a gun but never shot a deer. William Peters, owner of the camp where the men stayed said that they took away eight deer but he didn't know where the two came from that were eaten at the camp.

The respondents were called in turn and each emphatically denied the allegations of the State. They maintained that they shot merely the quota allowed by law, two deer a piece. These were shipped to their several homes from Rockwood. Attorney William Folsom Merrill moved that the case be dismissed because of insufficient evidence to warrant a verdict. County Attorney Anderson objected and the court ruled it a prima Facie. Following the arguments by counsel, all four respondents were dismissed.

— **Independent Reporter, September 13, 1913**

Post Office Break In

The post office at Standish was broken into Monday night, the safe blown to pieces and the contents stolen. Postmaster Hartford estimates the loss in stamps at $100 while he lost some cash besides valuable papers. No clue to the burglars has yet been found.

— Oxford Democrat, May 8, 1906

Child Injured

The Portland Press learns that on Tuesday of last week a son, aged 4 years, of S. E. Wheeler of Standish, fell from a hay scaffold, a distance of nine feet, breaking one of his thighs, and otherwise severely injuring him. He is recovering.

— Lewiston Evening Journal July 24, 1867

Drowning

Standish.—The Portland Press states that a son of Wentworth Dresser of Standish, was drowned Thursday afternoon in Little Ossipee river while rafting a boom of logs. His body was recovered in 20 minutes, but all efforts to resuscitate life were fruitless. He was about 20 years of age. He fell between the logs and his head was jammed.

— Lewiston Evening Journal, May 11, 1872

Assault and Battery

Superior Court - April Term - Godard, J. Presiding

State vs. John Drost, George Harmon, and Leland S. Richardson. Indictment for assault and battery upon Savory, at Standish. On the fifth day of the term, Drost pleaded not guilty. To-day he retracted his plea and pleaded guilty. It appearing that he had already suffered two months imprisonment, he was sentenced to ten days imprisonment. Richardson was arraigned on the same indictment and pleaded nolo contendere. He was fined $5 and one third the costs at this Court.

Webb.   Swasey & Son.

— Portland Daily Press, May 19, 1869

Attempted Suicide

Standish.—Thomas Skillings, a pauper on the Standish poor farm, attempted suicide Thursday by hanging. After he was cut down he ran away with the rope and has not been seen since.

— **Lewiston Evening Journal, May 27, 1876**

Tornado in Standish

During the thunder of Tuesday afternoon, the 25th, ult., a destructive tornado occurred in the town of Standish, Cumberland county. The barns of D. Moulton, Mr. Shackford, and H. J. Swasey were unroofed; many elms and maples prostrated and broken to pieces, windows broken and sheds blown down. It passed through the orchards of A. W. Marrett and G. Howe and the garden of H. J. Swasey, uprooting and breaking into fragments many valuable fruit trees. A man at work in his field with his oxen and cart was taken up and hurled some ten rods—his cart overset and carried a long distance. Stone walls were blown down and the rocks blown to the distance of rods. Fragments of trees, weighing hundreds of pounds, were hurled through the air to the distance of thirty or forty rods.

— **Maine Farmer, October 4, 1860**

Fatal Mining Accident

Henry M. Weston and George C. Chadbourne, two industrious young men from Standish, Maine, lost their lives by the caving in of a bank near the Junction of the Middle Yaba.

— **Maine Democrat, March 22, 1853**

The Shooting Affair

The shooting affair, to which reference was made yesterday, creates quite a stir in town. Mr. Sanborn who so carelessly and harmlessly emptied the revolver at Mr. McIntire, is a sober, well-to-do farmer of Standish, about 34 years of age. The trouble is all about Miss Amanda Foss, who resides at the house of Mr. Sanborn, and who recently informed Mr. Sanborn that McIntire, some three years since, while the woman was living in Kennebunkport, by the means of threats and violence outraged her. Sanborn, whose seal is to be respected more than his discretion, took upon himself the task of bringing the alleged culprit to justice. His purpose seemed to be to cause McIntire to go to Standish and see the woman, but in order to have the means at hand to compel his victim to come to terms he went to Portland and bought a pistol and cartridges, then proceeded to Cape Elizabeth to practice in the art of gunnery: This done, he went in search of McIntire. After finding him, shaking hands with him, and telling him his errand, he says the latter agreed to go to Standish, but in a few minutes concluded he would see Miss Foss when she came to Saco, where McIntire lives. Sanborn seems to have lost his presence of mind, and immediately drew his pepper box and sent a'leaden shower after McIntire, who beat a hasty but safe retreat Sanborn was up before Judge Chase yesterday morning, who bound him over to the Supreme Court in $5000. He will probably get bail.

— Portland Daily Press, April 17, 1872

Frightened Oxen

A. Nason of Standish, was plowing with his oxen last Friday, when they became frightened, threw him down and ran over him, dragging the plow over his back. It is feared he is injured for life.

— Maine Farmer, May 31, 1873

Painful Accident

Jonathan Haskell, son of Francis Haskell of Standish, about 19 years of age, while engaged in sawing shingles on Friday last, had one of his hands taken off by the saw, as we learn from the Biddeford Gazette. A shingle got caught in the machine, and as Mr. H. stepped forward to stop it by shutting the gate, he made a misstep and in falling put out his hand to save himself, brought it in contact with the saw which severed it from the wrist instantly. So quick was it done that he was not aware of its loss till he reached out his arm to shut the gate, and turning towards the platform, beheld his hand lying thereon. This is a sad accident as this young man is the only son and sole dependence of his father who is infirm, and requires the aid of his son for support.

— Maine Farmer, June 24, 1858

Bonny Eagle Notes

To the Editor of the Press:

Your good paper has quite a large circulation around here, but still we are not permitted the opportunity of being noticed, not having any correspondent from this post office, to report the news, home happenings, etc., etc., as other places have. I can't perceive why this is the case, unless it is that no one has ever desired to become a reporter. I have been a subscriber to the Maine State Press for the past five years and do not feel at home without it every week. It is a welcome guest.

I subjoin the following items.

A few evenings ago the friends of Elder Frank Haines. (pastor of the church at Bonny Eagle) called at his residence and gave him a donation of $50 worth of provisions, household goods, and money.

Last Wednesday evening some vile wretches broke about a dozen panes of glass from the Methodist church at South Standish. No clue to the rascals has yet been obtained, but it is hoped that they may yet be found out and get what they so much deserve.

Alphonzo G. Davis, the young Advent preacher and stage driver, from West Buxton, has lately skedaddled and left his wife alone to grope her way in the world.

Business is quite brisk at Bonny Eagle. The lumbering firms of A. & E. B. Usher and I. L. Came are quite extensively engaged in box-shook making, the two mills turning out about 700 per day. No hard times yet. Zeph.

— **Portland Daily Press, November 24, 1875**

Arrest of a Thief

On Tuesday last, James L. Chase (a jeweler) from Boston, was arrested at Sebago Lake, in Standish, by Dept. Sheriff Dresser, on a charge of embezzlement of diamonds and jewelry of the value of several hundred dollars; Chase was accompanied to Boston on Monday evening by detective Dearborn of the Boston Police.

— **Portland Daily Press, July, 20, 1871**

Brutal Punishment

It is charged that Mr. Ellwin one of the Selectmen of Baldwin teaching school at Steep Falls, inhumanly whipped a little boy, by the name of Skillings, only eight years old, so that he had to be carried home, first brutally pulling his ears, then blistering both his hands, then taking him across his knee and pounding him to a jelly with a heavy ferrule. The poor boy is in critical condition.

— **Portland Daily Press, February 5, 1874**

Horse Stolen

A man who came from Standish to Portland on Saturday, with a valuable horse attached to a wagon, left his team for a few moments, when the horse was detached from the wagon and stolen.

— Maine Farmer, March 7, 1874

The Railroad Accident at Sebago Lake

The Directors of the Portland and Ogdensburg railroad, with Mr. Corser, one of the Railroad Commissioners, were at Sebago Lake yesterday, investigating the cause of the railroad accident of Wednesday afternoon. We understand that the blame for the collision rests with Mr. Dingley, the man who had charge of the gravel train; for written instruction had been given that no gravel trains should be allowed to run below the Lake station when extra or special trains were on the road. The injured men are in comfortable condition, and will all recover, their wounds being only flesh cuts and bruises. We are unable to ascertain their names. Mr. Loring, the engineer, had an almost miraculous escape from instant death. When the platform car was turned over and came down upon the engine, several large stones were thrown into the cab, and a stake of the car was driven two feet through the roof. A quantity of wood from the tender was thrown by the concussion on to the foot-board, surrounding the engineer with dangerous missiles. When the trains came together, the fireman jumped from the engine and was unhurt. Mr. Loring, at the same moment, sprang for the whistle and grasped the reversing lever, and by the time he had reversed the engine the worst was over. He escaped with a very few slight bruises.

— Portland Daily Press, June 30, 1871

A Sharp Robbery

Saturday night, an officer from Standish stopped at the Perry house who was in search of a man who had accomplished a sharp robbery. He went into a field on the farm of a Standish, on Wednesday afternoon, yoked up a pair of fat oxen that girted about seven feet, and drove them into Portland reaching the city at 10 a.m. Thursday. He then drove the cattle to Best's, in Westbrook, and sold them for about $200, took a note for the same, had it discounted at the First National Bank (we think it was), and cleared. The officer had been hunting for the cattle everywhere and finally traced them to Best's who bought them in good faith supposing they belonged to him.

— Portland Daily Press, August 23, 1880

Log Jam Accident

Chas. Meserve of Bar Mills, while endeavoring to break a jam of logs in the river at Steep Falls Thursday last, had his leg badly broken by being caught among the logs as the jam gave way. The broken limb was set by Dr. Lord of Limington, and the man is now comfortable. Mr. Meserve is a hard-working man and poor, and his fellow river drivers contributed a comfortable sum of money for his relief.

— Portland Daily Press, July 7, 1879

Sad Accident at East Baldwin

On Monday, three young men, aged about 17 years, Eddie Richardson and Freddie and Josie Jackson, twin brothers, came down from Boston to East Baldwin for a week's recreation, in the family of D. T. Richardson, intending to return on Saturday.

Friday, about 1 o'clock, while Eddie and Freddie were out sporting with their guns, the ramrod in Eddie's gun stuck and he remarked he should have to blow it out. Freddie thought they could draw it, and took hold of the rod, while Eddie held the gun by the breech. The gun was loaded, and, as it happened, was cocked. The gun was discharged and the rod driven entirely through the body, holding only by the button on the end. The boy, holding the rod (iron rod) in his hand, walked a mile to Dr. James Norton's, where he lay on the lounge and had the rod removed by the aid of a lance without flinching. Dr. Norton removed the rod. Dr. Charles Maberry was soon in attendance, and, in about two hours, Dr. Cobb of Standish.

The rod passed very near the large intestine and the bladder, but it is hoped neither of them was hit. Saturday morning the boy had rested well the night previous and his pulse was 90. Sunday there was no great swelling compared with the severity of the wound.

— Portland Daily Press, August 1, 1881

Another Horse Thief

Steals a Portland Team, but the Owner Recovers It.

A week ago last Wednesday a man hired a team from J. B. Clark & Sons on Tyng street, for the purpose of canvassing for several days. It seems that he sold the team in Standish to Mr. Charles Thompson. A few days after Mr. Thompson purchased the horse, the animal got away in the night and came back to his old home with nothing on but a halter. Mr. Clark saw the advertisement in the Press, which Mr. Thompson put in describing the horse and supposing the name signed to it was that of the man who hired the team, took the horse to Standish. What was his surprise on arriving at Mr. Thompson's house to find that he claimed the horse as his own, having purchased him of the stranger; but as soon as matters were explained, Mr. Thompson willingly gave up the team to its rightful owners.

Nothing had been heard of the man who hired the team. He is described as an elderly man, very ministerial looking, and seemed to be all right. Mr. Thompson purchased the team at a very low price, but would not have bought it at all had not the man appeared to be all right. He represented that he bought the team at Bath, and had been stopping with Mr. Mitchell in Freeport. Mr. Mitchell says that no such person has been there.

— Portland Daily Press October 1, 1884

Mysteries of Sebago Lake

Sad Drowning Accident In It's Waters.
The First Recovery of a Human Body from Its Depths.

Your mention of the recovery of the body of Fred Murch from the waters of Sebago Lake calls to my mind similar drowning accidents within my recollection. Young Murch was drowned on the ninth of May by the upsetting of a boat near the Dingley Islands. The boat contained three young men. Augustus Jordan spent his strength in assisting the others, and after swimming ashore on an island, died of exhaustion. Albert, a brother of the Murch who was drowned could not swim, but saved his life by hanging on to the boat.

The death of these young men caused much excitement in their town of Casco, and large numbers of men with all the usual appliances dragged the bottom of the lake for several days for the body of the drowned boy, but with little hope of success, as the elder people discouraged them, arguing that from some mysterious property the water of the lake retained whatever was sunk in it. No result rewarded their labors, nor did the body rise to the surface at the time they usually do in other waters.

After three weeks from the drowning an experienced diver was employed who went down in nearly one hundred feet of water, and searched four hours among boulders, and on the following morning, after a thorough search of the lake, walking eight miles, he stepped on the body of the drowned boy. It was found to be in a good, state of preservation and nearly covered by sediment. This drifting sediment, by its covering the bodies, may be the cause why they are not found. This is said to be the first body ever recovered from the deep waters of the lake, although they reach a much greater depth further from the shore.

In confirmation of the assertion that there is a mysterious property in the waters in the depths of the lake which retains everything which reaches it, I will narrate a more serious accident on the lake, which occurred nearly sixty years ago, of which I have a distinct recollection. In the early days of the powder manufacture at Gambo Falls, Windham, the business was carried on by the firm of Edmond Fowler & Co., which was composed of two Fowler brothers from Southwick, Mass., and Lester Laflin of the same State. On the 22nd of June, 1828, Edmond Fowler, Laflin, and their foreman, Matthew McCulley. went to Chadbourne's landing in Standish for a sail on the lake. Near the landing lived William Horr, who with Chadbourne owned a large clinker-built sail boat thirty-five feet long, schooner rigged and carrying a jib. The boat was named the Ellen, and had been kept as a pleasure boat in Portland harbor. Her masts were very long, and she was considered unsafe. She finally capsized and drowned the Bangs brothers, when she was sold and taken to the lake. Horr was an experienced boatman, and readily engaged to take the Fowler party up the lake, and also took his own son of some thirteen years with him. The party left in good spirits. The circumstances of the reappearance of the boat and the sad fate of the party 1 received some years ago from a son of Mr. Chadbourne's, who owned a part of the boat, and from Mrs. Bodge who was Esther Harmon, a sister of the wife of Horr, the boatman. She was then thirteen, and lived in their family on the high shore of the lake, overlooking its sea-like expanse. Henry Chadbourne, now dead, said that an hour before sunset a small very dark cloud appeared in the west, and gradually arose against the wind as it blew over the lake. The threatening appearance of the cloud caused her father to look for the sailing party. The boat was discovered far up the take. She had all sail set with a stiff breeze from the east; she was on the starboard tack close hauled and apparently striving to fetch the landing before the squall struck.

Mrs. Bodge said that at the time the gale struck she was returning from the well several rods from the house, and in sight of the lake. Her path was through a piece of winter wheat which was fully grown. She was not expecting the gale to strike so soon, when she heard the howl of the tempest on the lake, and thought she heard scream from the same direction at the same time. A fearful flash of lightning surrounded her, and did not immediately disappear. She heard no thunder but the gale came with the lightning. She was frightened and imagined the waving grain was water through which she was wading, but on reaching the house her clothes were perfectly dry. Before the air became thick, the boat was seen between Sticky river point and Indian Island, in the open water seen in looking north from the present railroad landing. Night immediately shut down with no appearance of the party, but not much alarm was felt as it was supposed that the boat was driven on to the sandy beach of the island.

The next morning a party in a boat was sent, who found on the shore of the island four hats and an oar, but no other signs of the boat or the party.

It was apparent to all that when the wind, which brought the cloud, suddenly overcame the wind from the east which was then filling the sails, the boat was upset and her stone ballast carried her at once to the bottom.

The neighboring settlements were immediately alarmed and a search was begun with boats and rafts, and for many days that part of the lake was thoroughly dragged with all kinds of grapnels, and although the masts of the boat had shrouds. no grapnel took hold of them. At the end of two weeks "the head-works," a timber structure with a house and a capstan on it, used to warp rafts of logs the lake, was brought round from the outlet, and anchored over the supposed spot of the accident. An effort was made to raise the bodies by the jar of heavy guns. A cannon was brought from Portland and placed on the headworks, and for several days the mournful guns kept the people excited within a circle of ten miles. When in ordinary warm water, gases form in a human body, and it rises to the surface. When about to float, the jar produced by the firing of cannon sometimes loosens the body from the bottom and hastens the rising, but in the case of the

Fowler party no such result followed, nor probably will not until "the sea gives up its dead." The mystery of the lake is probably its great depth of very cold water, which no warm current reaches, and all matter sunk in it remains the same.

The scene of the search for the bodies of the Fowler party was made the more painful from the presence of the brothers and friends of Mr. Fowler; the young wife of Mr. Laflin, to whom he had been married but a few weeks, and the wife of the boatman Horr, who for a long life looked from her window across the lake each night for the coming of her husband and son. W. G.

— **Portland Daily Press, June 9, 1886**

Dirty Laundry

Before Judge Lane

Thursday.—Betsey Thorne vs. Solomon Schien.— Action on account annexed for working 87 weeks it one dollar per week. Defendant with his three brothers, who are German pedlars, boarded at the plaintiff's house in Standish, paying therefor twenty cents a meal. Plaintiff says that Solomon told her if she would do their washing and mending he would pay her for it. Solomon and his brothers testified that the washing was to be included in the board which had been settled for. Jury trial was waived and cause tried by the Judge. Decision for the plaintiff for amount claimed. Swasey & Son. Scribner

Harnesses Taken

H. B. Hartford's store at Standish, was broken into Sunday night and about $100 worth of harnesses taken.

— Portland Daily Press, August 15, 1893

Wheeling Away

**Two Young Massachusetts Fellows Were
So Doing When Constable Murch Pursued**

Last evening, Constable Josiah Murch of Standish brought to the police station two young men, aged about 20 years each, whom he had arrested for stealing two bicycles from a man in Standish. The names of the young men were given by them last evening as Charles Young of Springfield, Mass., and Fred Fletcher of Boston. They had been visiting an aunt of Young's in that part of the country, and took the machines to help them back to Boston. Constable Murch pursued them eight miles yesterday and overtook them. Fletcher said last night that he did not intend to steal the machine, but Young was disposed to be more frank and admit the whole. They will be brought before the court Wednesday.

— Portland Daily Press, May 1, 1894

Stolen

STOLEN from the Subscriber in Standish, on the night of July 18, 1882, a Red Mare, about eight years old, black mane and tail, two white hind feet, shackle on left hind foot, left hip slightly started. Whoever will give information, or return said Mare, will be suitably rewarded. REUBEN HARMON Sebago Lake, July 20, 1882.

— Portland Daily Press, July 24, 1882

A Peculiar Case

**John Kohler Arrested on Suspicion of
Murdering G. Fred Harmon.
An Analysis of Mr. Harmon's Stomach Necessary.
The Motive for Such a Crime in Doubt.**

Yesterday afternoon Deputy Marshal Crowel arrested John Kohler, on suspicion of causing the death of Mr. G. Fred Harmon in this city in February last; Mr. Kohler, who was on the way to his boarding house, No. 47 Myrtle street, when the Deputy told him he was wanted, turned and accompanied the Deputy to the station. The reporters for the Press, on hearing of the affair, interviewed the following persons and received the accompanying information:

THE MARSHAL'S ACCOUNT

Marshal Andrews spent the evening in his office. In conversation with a reporter, he said that Kohler claims to be 40 years of age, says he was born in Cayenne, French Guiana, of a German father and French mother; that he is a hat molder by trade, and came to this country from Cayenne about eleven years ago. He came to Portland about two years ago and engaged with Wm. H. Somers, the Middle street hatter, for whom he worked some time, when he went to Boston and remained there until he returned to Portland in October last, when he again entered Mr. Somers's employ. Mr. Somers went to San Francisco, and promised him, he said, that when he returned he would raise his (Kohler's) pay. Mr. Somers did not keep his promise, and so, about four weeks ago, Kohler left his employ and has been doing nothing since. He engaged board in this city at No. 47 Myrtle street, a boarding house kept by Mrs. G. Fred Harmon, Mr. Somers assisting him in procuring this boarding place. A week ago he went to Boston to procure work, but returned to Portland, and when arrested last night his trunk was packed, as he intended to visit Boston again when arrested.

While Kohler was boarding at No. 47 Myrtle street, Mr. Harmon, the husband of the lady who keeps the house, was taken sick and was under the care of Dr. James Buzzell, and later under the care of Dr. A. V. Thompson. While the latter was attending him, Dr. Gerrish was called in for consultation. The doctors treated their patient for gastritis, but their medicines failed of the desired effect. They were puzzled, for they could not see why the man did not get well. On February 22d Harmon died suddenly. The doctors desired a postmortem examination, which Mrs. Harmon seemed willing to have made, but later she objected, the reason given being that Mr. Harmon's aged parents, who lived in Standish, were opposed to the cutting up of the body. Mr. Harmon had been sickly, had had a severe rheumatic attack two years ago, which had paralyzed one arm. The Marshal, on being asked what motive, if any, Kohler could have had in murdering Harmon—provided the suspicions were true—couldn't say. He did not believe there had been any connection of Mrs. Harmon with the murder, provided any murder had been committed. Only three days ago was it ascertained that Kohler had been buying arsenic, for which he seemed to have no use. If the stomach of the deceased should be exhumed and its contents analyzed, showing arsenic therein, then suspicion of Kohler, in his opinion, would be very strong. Mr. Harmon, the deceased, was born in Standish, was a carpenter by trade, but had not done much work since his disablement.

THE PRISONER

While the reporter was at the station, Kohler was brought out of the cell, and appeared an olive complexioned fellow, with black moustache and hair, keen eye, an erect carriage, and is said to be apparently a shrewd, bright fellow.

DR. BUZZELL'S STATEMENT

Dr. James Buzzell was the first physician called. Kohler came to his house on the morning of the 4th of February and said that Harmon was sick and wished to see him. Dr. Buzzell visited the house and found that Harmon was suffering, as he supposed, from bilious emesis. He gave the customary remedies for stomach disorder and repeated his visits almost daily until the twelfth when Dr. Thompson, who was the Harmon's' family physician, took charge of the case. It seems that Harmon had been deprived of the use of his arm by a large abscess which had been under treatment during the past two years, and he imagined that this might have been the source of the trouble. In describing the manner in which he was taken ill to the doctor on the occasion of his first visit, Harmon remarked that he had first felt sick directly after drinking his coffee in the morning. Dr. Buzzell did not regard the case as serious and was greatly surprised when he learned of Harmon's death. He said that Kohler appeared to be in complete charge of the sick room and impressed him as a kind man. He made, to all appearances, a good hire and seemed on the best of terms with his patient. Dr. Buzzell knew both Mr. and Mrs. Harmon, having lived near them both before and after their marriage.

The Doctor said that although he thought of nothing irregular at the time, the symptoms of Harmon's illness were like those of poisoning. During the illness, Mrs. Harmon appeared to be suffering from a severe cold and sat in an adjoining room to that of her husband.

DR. THOMPSON'S STATEMENT

Dr. A. V. Thompson, who attended Harmon, was seen last night, and stated that he was first called on Feb. 12th, and attended Harmon until the 22d, when the man died. Dr. Thompson found

Harmon suffering with inflammation of the stomach accompanied by severe vomiting. He pronounced the sickness to be gastritis, and applied the usual remedies.

On the 14th and 16th days of February, Dr. Frederic Henry Gerrish visited the patient in company with Dr. Thompson, and concurred in his opinion of the case. It was thought that Harmon would recover, provided there was no disorganization of the stomach and other organs. From the time the physician made his first visit until his last on the evening before the death, there was nothing to cause any serious apprehensions of a fatal result. The temperature was bit slightly above the natural degree, and the pulse only slightly accelerated.

On Saturday evening, at about half past eight, when the doctor made his last visit, the patient complained of feeling paralyzed from his throat downward and was very thirsty, but although the change was slightly for the worse, no danger was apprehended and Dr. Thompson left the house, supposing that his patient was comfortable. The next morning, Sunday, the 22d, the doctor was telephoned just after breakfast that Harmon had died.

When Dr. Thompson made his first call he found Kohler in charge of the sick room, and he was present with two exceptions at all the doctor's calls. He seemed on good terms with his patient. Mrs. Harmon was sometimes in the room. Dr. Thompson did not see her carry on any extended conversation with Kohler, nor notice any intimacy between them. Kohler apparently followed the doctor's directions, in administering the medicine.

Dr. Thompson called at the house Sunday forenoon after being notified of the death. He thought it strange that Harmon should have died so suddenly when he had left him in no apparent danger the night before. With a view to ascertaining the cause of the sudden disease of the patient, Dr. Thompson said to Mrs. Harmon that he would like to make a postmortem examination. Kohler, who was in the room, said that it would amount to nothing only to satisfy the physicians. Mrs. Harmon expressed herself as being perfectly willing to allow the autopsy to take place as far as she herself was concerned, but added that she thought the old folks, Harmon's parents, would object. The physician did not press his point, as he had asked for the autopsy only to satisfy his curiosity as to the cause of a sudden and somewhat inexplicable death. At this time, Dr. Thompson had no apprehension of anything wrong, his suspicions being first aroused when he afterwards learned of Kohler's purchase of arsenic at the time of the sickness.

In response to a question as to whether or not the symptoms of Harmon showed the presence of arsenic in the system, Dr. Thompson said that there were symptoms—such as a burning feeling and intense thirst—which might indicate the presence of arsenic in the system, but which might also be nothing but the natural accompaniments of the disease.

Dr. Thompson has known both Mr. and Mrs. Harmon for a number of years, and spoke of them as honest and respectable persons. He added that he saw nothing in the conduct of Kohler in the sick room to arouse suspicion.

MR. CHRISTOPHER WAY'S STATEMENT

Mr. Christopher Way, the apothecary on the corner of Myrtle and Cumberland streets, of whom Mr. Kohler is supposed to have bought arsenic, was called upon by a Press reporter and asked the dates of the alleged purchases. Mr. Way declined to give any information unless the Marshal first gave his consent. He took down a book—probably containing a record of the sales of poisons—and with the reporter proceeded to the Marshal's office, but the Marshal refused to give his consent. It is stated, however, on what appears to be good authority, that Mr. Kohler purchased arsenic at five different times, saying that he intended to use it in coloring hat bands. Mr. Way did not deny that he had sold Mr. Kohler arsenic.

MR. SOMERS' STORY

Mr. W. H. Somers of the hat firm of Somers & Co., 253 Middle street, was called open last night, and in response to questions regarding Kohler, made substantially the following statement:

"John W. Kohler entered our employ Oct. 4th, 1884, as a journeyman hatter, and he was with us till the following March. The man was a fair workman and regular at his work. Kohler is a French Portuguese. The only peculiarity about him that I noticed was that he had a very quick temper. While he was at work for us, Fred Harmon and his wife called at the store frequently to see Kohler, and the husband appeared to be on very intimate terms with him. At one time, Kohler requested us to take Harmon into the shop and teach him the trade, to which we objected, and the conversation on this matter came near resulting in Kohler's leaving our employ. After Mr. Harmon's death Mrs. Harmon came to the shop several times."

During the conversation the reporter asked Mr. W. H. Somers if he used arsenic in his business and received a reply in the negative. "What, do you not color hat bands with it?"

"No, sir, I do not use it at all; neither have I used it on hat bands nor anything else. All of my hat bands are purchased in New York direct of an importer."

Kohler's quick temper had a tendency to make him somewhat unpopular with the other workmen, some of whom it is said delighted in hectoring him. It has been reported that at one time, in a fit of anger, Kohler chased a workman down stairs with a hatchet in his hand, but Mr. Somers said he did not see any such transaction. He, however, declined to say that Kohler left the firm's employ of his own accord.

FOR ANALYSIS

It is reported that the body of Mr. Harmon will be exhumed at Standish today and the stomach sent to Prof. Carmichael, at Brunswick, for analysis.

— **Portland Daily Press, May 23, 1885**

A Gang of Swindlers

**Four Men Arrested Last Night
as Suspicious Characters
They Had Various Gambling Devices
Young Boston Men - Have Been Here a Week
"Cute" McGinty Arrested with Them.**

Early last evening, when Officers Madden and White returned from Sebago Lake, they brought to the police station two young men. Later, Officer Frith arrived from Sebago Lake with another young man. Later still, Officer Frank arrived from Sebago Lake with another young man. Meanwhile, another officer brought in "Cute" McGinty a well-known character about this city. These were all arrested as suspicious characters, and supposed to be members of a gang of six or seven that have been in this city about a week, making it the base of operations in all gatherings in this vicinity, such as the Labor Day excursion to Sebago Lake, where they work all sorts of games of chance and any kind of deceit to make a dollar. The first two had with them a peculiar gambling device. Three bright heavy rows of some white metal revolved on a pivot. When set in the middle of a large disc with numbers and revolved it constituted a gambling machine.

The third young man had several pairs of eye-glasses, apparently gold-bowed, where with he had been playing the famous spectacles trick, by saying that he had found a pair of gold-bowed spectacles and offering to sell them cheap. Another device was an arrangement whereby a ball could be made to drop into different colored slots.

It looks as if the police had captured some very pernicious people, and had broken up a gang of swindlers and shell men. A Portland man lost a gold watch and some money at Sebago Lake yesterday, and one of the arrested men knows something about them, he thinks.

— Portland Daily Press, September 4, 1894

Local News

Henry Redlon of Bog Mills, Buxton, an employee of Amos Boulter of Standish, while "setting up" a threshing machine at the barn of Henry Hasty of this town (Limington), last week, caught a hook in his thigh near the groin tearing a frightful wound.

Mr. George Meserve of Limerick lost a valuable cow last week by her walking through a piece of fallen growth and catching the "hind foot" in a crutch, and being unable to extricate it, was thrown down hill, and failing to come up with the cattle at night, was found early the following morning in the above condition, dead.

Mr. Joseph Harmon of Bonny Eagle was blasting rocks one day last week; one charge failing to explode from imperfect fuse, Mr. Harmon undertook to drill out the "tamping" and as the drill punched through into the powder, the powder took fire, throwing the drill and sledge some twenty rods. Mr. Harmon narrowly escaped serious injury, as quite a quantity of powder was blown into bis face,

— Portland Daily Press, October, 13, 1882

A Runaway at Westbrook

Two Teams and Four Men Badly Mixed Up

Yesterday afternoon a bad runaway occurred in Westbrook. Gilbert C. Davis and Edward Morton started from Portland to drive to Standish. When at the East End, the horse became alarmed at a passing car and became unmanageable. Davis leaped out and seized the horse by the reins. At the same time, a carriage driven by Dr. Smith, who had as company Treasurer Woodman of the bank, approached. The horse made a dash, colliding with Dr. Smith's team, which was upset, and both horses were thrown down. Davis, still clinging to the horse's head, was crashed in the tangle and was taken out in a badly demoralized condition. Morton, who is man well advanced in years, was thrown from the seat and received bad bruises. The occupants of the other team escaped injury. The offending animal got on its legs again and bolted up Main street finding a clear course until he collided with S.D. Warren's stock house, breaking a shaft and driving the end of it for a foot and a half into its body, probably putting an end to its career. The horse belonged to M. S. Spear of Standish.

Mr. Davis was badly injured, having, two ribs fractured and breaking the bone of his leg above the ankle.

— Portland Daily Press, September 22, 1894

The Tramp's Hotel

Much Damage Caused in the
Standish School House at Steep Falls.

Saturday, a tramp made a great deal of trouble in the Standish school house at Steep Falls. The tramp made a lodging house of the school house Saturday night, and in order to keep warm built a fire in the stove. There was plenty of wood; but with a stupid perversity, the tramp preferred to use the school books for fuel. He also treated the school house shamefully, and took a large number of the pens and pencils of the pupils. The whole damage will be about fifty dollars. The teacher of the school, Mr. George Bragdon of Limington, started in pursuit as soon as the vandalism was discovered. In Limington, he overtook the tramp, and invited him to ride. To return the compliment, the tramp offered him some pencils and penholders. One bore the name of Tom Wingate, one of the scholars.

The tramp was delivered to Constable H. Sawyer of Limington, who had him put under guard at the poor farm.

Monday Deputy Sheriff Dolloff of Steep Falls, came to Portland and got a warrant. The tramp will be brought before the

Portland Municipal court Wednesday morning. He is about forty-five years of age.

— Portland Daily Press, February 19, 1895

GRADE SCHOOL, STEEP FALLS, ME.

A Sunday Suicide at Standish

Standish, April 21. —South Standish, a little village situated about four miles from Standish village, was thrown into a wild state of excitement about 3:30 Sunday afternoon. Mr. Thomas Davis, who claimed Saco as his home, but who was born in South Standish, was at Orville S. Sanborn's, a citizen of that place, when the family were attracted by a loud report. Mr. Sanborn, ongoing to the shed, found the body of Mr. Davis lying with a bullet hole through his temple. He was about 50 years of age. He has been a surveyor of timber for a great many years. He was well-to-do, and it was a great surprise to his many friends. Melancholia was the cause of the deed. He leaves a widow.

— Portland Daily Press, April 22, 1895

Beer Seizure

Deputy Sheriff E. W. Dolloff, in company with Sheriff W. H. Dresser of Portland, made a big haul Wednesday night at Sebago Lake. The incoming train from Portland brought about fifteen barrels of lager beer, and the sheriffs, thinking this would be the case, was all prepared and confiscated the lot and locked it up; as there was no claimant no arrests were made. This is the first seizure that was ever made at this place, and it was certainly a shrewd piece of work on the part of the sheriffs. Give us a few more such men and we will show you what the prohibitory law can do.

— Portland Daily Press, July 6, 1895

Robbery at Standish

Quite a little excitement occurred at the Village Tuesday morning over a tramp. The facts as near as could be ascertained are these: A man giving his name as Adams of Boston asked permission to step into Geo. R. Thompson's stable. This was about 7:30. Mr. Thompson gave him permission and stepped out of the stable. In the meantime Mr. Thompson's vest hung on a nail and in one of the pockets a $10 bill. Of course it did not escape the tramp's keen eye. When Mr. Thompson came back the tramp and $10 were missing. Thinking the tramp must have taken it, he notified Deputy Sheriff Dolloff and together they started in pursuit of the intruder. They overtook him about four miles from the village and brought him back, he protesting all the while that he knew nothing about it. Sheriff Dolloff took his prisoner to Portland and made a thorough search. By taking off the man's stocking the $10 bill rolled onto the floor. The tramp's explanation was that he got it in Boston. He will be obliged to answer to a charge of larceny in the municipal court.

— Portland Daily Press, May, 30, 1895

A Serious Charge

A Well Known Farmer of Standish Accused of a Murderous Assault

Yesterday morning In the Municipal court, an interesting assault case was taken up in which two citizens of Standish were interested.

Deputy Sheriff Robert F. Newhall came to the city in the morning bringing with him Eliab Blake, seventy years of age. Blake wore old fashioned ear rings, and has a long snow white beard. Albert E. Shaw, the plaintiff, is about sixty years old.

After Recorder Turner read the warrant charging Blake with assault, he answered by saying, "I ain't guilty"

This is the story of the case:

On the afternoon of the day stated in the complaint, Shaw visited the home of Blake. The former had heard that the old gentleman had been circulating stories to the effect that he had been drunk around the village quite a good deal of late. He wished Blake to deny this, in short to make an apology. Blake however stood his grounds and instead of appeasing the wrath of Shaw, served rather to increase the anger. One word led to another until at last both becoming so excited, Blake is alleged to have seized a stick and hit his unwelcome visitor. Things grew worse. Blake followed up by taking a knife with which he made a keen thrust upon Shaw. The latter warded off the blow with his left hand and that member received a severe cut, the blood flowing profusely.

Things had begun to reach a most dangerous pass and Shaw evidently thinking discretion the better part of valor, concluded to start for home. He was just getting out of the yard when Blake called him to come back. Shaw had no desire of doing this. Then Blake took a two barreled shot gun and when Shaw turned and looked back at him, he discharged the full contents. The charge was a heavy one and the shot planted itself into many portions of Shaw's frame. His face was well peppered while the wounds received in the abdomen and legs were so severe as to cause him to call upon Dr. Harper of Windham.

These facts became known to County Attorney True and by his direction Blake was arrested and brought into court yesterday morning.

Assistant County Attorney Webb appeared for the prosecution and Henry W. Swasey for Blake. It was decided, as a continuance was desired, to continue the case to Friday, August 9th. Bail was furnished for Blake in the sum of $1000 by Blake himself and George L. Warren of this city. Mr. Shaw is a well-known farmer and always had an excellent reputation.

— **Portland Daily Press, August 1, 1895**

The Shaw-Blake Case Dismissed

In the Municipal Court yesterday morning the case of Albert Shaw vs. Eliab Blake was brought up and settled. This is the so-called Standish shooting case, wherein Blake was alleged to have used a shotgun on Shaw. The complaint made against Blake, however, was for simple assault, and in such cases the aggrieved party may file an acknowledgment of satisfaction. This, Mr. Shaw did, so the case was dismissed. Swasey appeared for Blake, and Solders & Chase for Shaw.

— Portland Daily Press, August 10, 1895

The Sebago Lake Rioters

Workmen are engaged in repairing in the Municipal Court room ceiling that was damaged by the recent bursting of the tank in City Hall, so Judge Robinson held his court yesterday morning in the officers room of the police station. There was an accumulation of business since Friday of last week, so the unfortunates had to be brought in from the cell room in relays.

The most important cases were those of Fred J. Larkin and Edwin Lowry, arraigned for felonious assault on Officer Robert F. Newhall at Sebago Lake on Labor Day. Carroll W. Morrill, Esq., appeared for Larkin, and Assistant County Attorney Webb was present for the State. The prisoners made no defense and the only question was one of bail.

Judge Robinson said that he would not assume jurisdiction, but would find probable cause and bind the men over to the Superior Court.

Mr. Morrill, Esq., asked that the bail might be fixed at an amount within the means of those who might give bail for Larkin.

Judge Robinson did not think $600 sufficient ball, and suspended decision until he could ascertain whether the cases of the two men were likely to come before the grand jury now in session.

Judge Robinson continued the case against each for one week, fixing the bail of each at $800. The object of this is probably to keep the men in custody until the grand jury shall act in the case.

Lowry pleaded guilty, and in default of bail was committed. Larkin, who pleaded not guilty, got bonds, his father and Edgar E. Rounds furnishing the bail.

— **Portland Daily Press, September 5, 1895**

Charged with Arson

**William Archibald of Standish Under Arrest.
It Is Alleged That He Set Fire to Clarence Ridlon's Barn
He Declares That He Was Far Away From
the Scene of the Fire.**

Yesterday afternoon Deputy Sheriff Dolloff of Standish, arrested and brought to this city William Archibald, on a charge of setting fire to the barn of Clarence Ridlon, in Standish, on Wednesday afternoon last.

The end of April, Mr. Ridlon hired Archibald, who is a young man, to work on the farm for three months. During that time, Archibald worked well. When the time expired, on July 31, Mr. Ridlon told him he had no further use for his services. Archibald, however, remained about the place, living on Mr. Ridlon and spending his time playing ball and reading in his room instead of doing chores about the place in return for his living. Mr. Ridlon then told him he couldn't expect to live there if he didn't work.

Last Tuesday, Mr. Ridlon told Archibald to go and Archibald went off. Wednesday afternoon, the barn was discovered to be in flames and was entirely consumed together with a quantity of hay and some hogs, The barn and contents were valued at $1000, on which there was $500 Insurance.

It was at once believed from the time at which the fire started and from other clues in the possession of Mr. Dolloff, that Archibald must have been the incendiary. He was found by Mr. Dolloff and arrested. Archibald claimed to be able to prove an alibi saying that at the time of the fire he was away in Boston. Deputy Sheriff Dolloff, however, says he has got the incendiary sure; that he has traced him from the time he left Standish on Tuesday to the time of the fire the next afternoon. Archibald is now in jail.

Mr. Ridlon will feel the loss of his property very keenly. Some five years ago he met a severe pecuniary loss and had just succeeded In getting on his feet again.

— Portland Daily Press, September 5, 1896

Charged with Incendiarism

**Wm. Archibald of Standish Accused of
Burning Clarence Ridlon's Barn.**

Portland, Sept. 4.—William Archibald of Standish, was arrested, today, charged with setting fire to the barn of Clarence Ridlon of that place. Wednesday afternoon. Archibald had been employed as a farm hand by Ridlon three months and was discharged. July 31. He remained about the farm doing nothing until Tuesday when Ridlon told him to leave.

Wednesday, Ridlon's barn was burned with a quantity of hay and some hogs, the loss being $1,000. Archibald was suspected and arrested by Sheriff Dolloff and brought to Portland, today, He claims an alibi.

— Daily Kennebec Journal, September 5, 1896

Attempted Arson
at Sebago Lake

Sebago Lake House came near burning Sunday morning. As Mr. Murch went in the stable, he found it all on fire and the well stopped up so there could not be any water got, but they put it out without its doing very much damage.

— Portland Daily Press, November 11, 1896

Another attempt was made last week to burn the Sebago Lake House. The incendiaries took a piece of board and bored a hole in it and put a candle in it, then covered the board with oil and then lighted the candle. Fortunately the candle went out before reaching the oil.

— **Portland Daily Press, January 6, 1897**

A Forgotten Tragedy of Standish Village

Detailed Story of the Murder of James Wooster
by John Clark 153 Years Ago Revealed
by Records of York County
and Early Suffolk Court Files in Boston.

One Sabbath morning, the 13th of March 1757, one hundred and fifty three years ago; the little frontier settlement of Pearsonstown, now Standish, Maine, was startled by an event which from its fatal consequences must have caused great excitement among the settlers of the neighboring towns of Buxton (Narragansett No. 1), Gorham and Falmouth and furnished a topic of lively interest for all the settlements from Kittery to Falmouth Neck. So far as is known to the writer, there exists no published account of the details of this tragedy nor of the causes leading up to it.

In the journal of the Rev. Thomas Smith of the First Church of Falmouth, under date of March 13, 1757 we find the following fact recorded: "One Clark, of Sebago-town, killed Wooster and wounded Gray and Sands." No further mention is made of the affair nor does the editor of this invaluable diary attempt to throve any light on the subject. McLellan, in his sketch of the Meserve family in the History of Gorham, refers to this entry in Smith's journal and concludes with the statement that "the history of these persons, or what the cause of the affray was, is now lost." After diligent search among the records of York County and the Early Suffolk Court Files in Boston, the story of this forgotten tragedy is revealed.

It seems that Elizabeth Clark, the widow of Eleazer Clark of Wells, Me., on the night of March 9th, 1757 had "stolen or taken away" from off the fence of the enclosure near the well by her dwelling house, one cotton and linen shift, several linen caps, one cotton and linen pillow-bier and several other things. The following Friday, the 11th of March, she made a complaint to John Storer, Justice of the Peace, who issued a warrant for the arrest of the person or persons in whose custody the goods should be found and delivered it to Alexander Gray, a deputy sheriff of York County. He, having reason to suspect that a Scotchman by the name of John Clark had stolen the goods, set out through the wilderness for the latter's home in Pearsontown. On the way he was joined by several others; at Biddeford by Joshua Mattocks, a blacksmith; at Narragansett No. 1 by Ephraim Sands, a carpenter the same who later built the house of the Rev. Paul Coffin; at Pearsontown, by Abraham York, James Wooster and Elijah Dunham, the latter one of the men stationed at the new fort, built two years before near the center of the present village of Standish. Early Sunday morning, the 13th of March, the party appeared before

Clark's dwelling house, armed with pistols, cutlasses and axes. They found the doors closed and securely barred. The records state that "Gray then informed Clark that he was an Officer and that he had a warrant from a Justice of the Peace to search for the stolen goods, and desired Clark to suffer him to come into the house to search for them and would have shown and read the warrant to him had he desired it, that Clark denied the officer entrance to his house and took down his gun and swore by his Maker that he would shoot the officer "if he did not go off." Thereupon they attempted to enter by force but were fired upon by Clark. Gray and Sands were "grievously wounded," and James Wooster "received upon his right thigh a mortal wound eight inches long and half an inch wide, of which mortal wound he then and there instantly died." During the excitement following the shooting and while the minds of the uninjured were intent upon caring for their dying comrade, Clark put on his snowshoes and escaped into the woods. The distressing scene may well be imagined—this solitary dwelling on the outskirts of civilization, the savage defiance of the besieged frontiersman, derisive shouts of the besiegers and the body of their slain comrade, stretched upon the snow, the terror of the two small children as they witnessed the ruthless struggle and the consternation of the women as they beheld its fatal termination.

As quickly as the slow traveling of the time of year permitted, Enoch Freeman and Moses Pearson of Falmouth, Justices of the Peace, were informed of the details of the tragedy they issued a warrant for the arrest of John Clark, his wife and daughter

Mary and delivered it to Brice McLellan, constable of the Town of Falmouth, who at once visited the scene of the crime, made the arrest and returned with the prisoners the next day. He also summoned Mr. Abraham York, Elijah Dunham and Mr. Joshua Mattocks as evidence.

Tuesday, March 15. "inquisition was held at Sebago Town, alias Pearson and Hobbs Town, before Joshua Bangs, gentleman, one of the coroners of York County upon the body of James Wooster of Sebago Town. Eleven of the men serving on the jury were from Gorham, two from Falmouth, and one from Sebago Town. The original document giving an account of the proceedings is an interesting one. Each of the jurors signed his own name and affixed to the document his seal, a large diamond-shaped piece of paper held firmly in place by a generous supply of sealing wax. The Gorham men on the jury were the first settlers of the town and lived in Gorham Village or immediate vicinity. They were Capt. John Phinney and Hugh McLellan, first two settlers of the town; Moses Akers, great grandfather of the sculptors, Charles and Paul Akers; Samuel Crockett, who built the two story house now standing on what is generally known as the Broad place on Main street in the village; John Freeman who lived on Fort Hill; Jacob Hamblen, whose home stood on the site of the present Narragansett Block; his son. Joseph Hamblen; William Lakeman, Benjamin Stevens, Joseph Weston and Nathaniel Whitney. The other three jurors were Anthony Brackett and Anthony Brackett, Jr., from Falmouth and John Burnell from the fort in Pearsonstown. The verdict of the Jury was that

"James Wooster was killed and came to his death by the hand of John Clark and that his wife and daughter were accessories thereunto." The total expense of the Inquest, including Coroner's and Constable's fees, travel, tailsmen, and Jurymen, was £2 16s 6d.

On the same day as the inquest, the two women, held in custody at Falmouth Neck, were brought before Enoch Freeman and Moses Pearson for examination. Jane Clark, when charged with "assisting and aiding husband in murdering James Wooster, Pearsontown, said that there were two guns shot by her husband, one through the door being partly open, that there were several men out of doors but did not know who he shot at, when the men came to the window she thought they came to press her husband, that she poked a pole out of the window to keep them off and that she did not make use of any other instrument but said pole." Her daughter Mary testified that "when the officer and men came up to the house they inquired for one Cole from the Army. Afterwards the officer, Mr. Gray, told them what he came for, that he had a Warrant against her father and asked him to deliver the stolen things, but he refused and got his gun and fired out of the window. Then the officer and men broke open the door with axes, and she beat them off with a stick and shut the door, one of the men being wounded in the arm. They broke open the door again part of the way, and the gun being loaded again her father put it out of the door, the men outside took hold of the gun and bent it, and then her father shot again and killed Wooster. The officer being wounded they left the door and her father made off." Evidently the wounds of Gray and Sands were not serious enough to prevent their being present at the examination. They and the other three men summoned as witnesses gave their evidence, "whereupon the mother and daughter were committed to the Jail in Falmouth there to be kept in custody until discharged by due course of Law."

In the meantime, the fugitive husband and father was endeavoring to make good his escape. Snow was falling when he plunged, blindly into the forest, a circumstance which made the task of pursuit much easier. For two days and two nights, he fled through the wilderness, without food and without sleep, constantly harassed by the fear of capture. He met no human being in his flight, save once when he was passing through York. He reached Kittery Tuesday evening where he tasted food for the first time since Sunday morning. His pursuers had displayed commendable activity, for the next day, March 16th, he was arrested in Kittery and taken to Simon Frost, Esq., for examination. He testified that "his name was John Clark and that he called himself Williams in order to avoid a Press Warrant, that he was born at Leith in the North of Scotland about the year 1707, about 16 years since he came from Scotland to Boston and that he lived at Nutfield for some years after his arrival at New England, that about 20 months ago they moved into the Eastern Country, that he has lived with his family at a place called Pearsontown about twelve months and has a wife and four children, and that he came from thence on account of a quarrel that arose between him and a man that called himself a King's Officer, that came with a number of men to take him last Sabbath Morning, that

the said Officer said he was come to take him and that he had
a Warrant so to do, and ordered him to open his door which
he delayed and immediately the Officer ordered them to knock
down the house, and that they began to cut down the door and
break it open, upon which he got his gun and put it through
the part of the door which was pried open and one of the men
took hold of the gun and went to pull it from him and the gun
discharged or was fired off. After which he got his hatchet and
went to the door and declared he would cut off the hand or finger
of any one who should come into the door, and made several
attempts or gave several blows for that purpose with the said
hatchet but is not sensible that he wounded anyone. At the same
time the people without struck at him with axes and a cutlass,
at length cut down the door and this examinent having fixed on
his snow shoes made his escape. A man in the company who
had a pistol in his hand told him to run for he had wounded a
man, accordingly he ran all day and the night following. It being
a snowy day, he says further that he had informed Mr. John Bane
and others of York of his circumstances as he came through, told
them that he had struck and wounded a man for which reason
he made his escape. The examinent further says upon the Officer
and this Company's coming he asked them what they came there
for and said Officer told him that he came to take him by the
Warrant before mentioned and he conceiving that he had not
committed any crime and so made his best defense and afterwards
his escape, that one Wooster happened at the same time to be
in the house and that the person who he supposed to be the

Officer asked the said Wooster whether he joined with Clark in resisting him and if he did not come out to them immediately, upon which the said Wooster upon the examinent's desire went up through the chimney, the said examinent further saith, that he has passed through the country without victuals or sleep from Sabbath morning till Tuesday evening, when he ate some victuals at Andrew Neal's at Kittery, after which he went to the House of Peter Whittom, Jr., where he was apprehended by virtue of a Warrant from Simon Frost, Esq."

The original document has been preserved and is signed by John Clark in his own handwriting and attested by Simon Frost, Justice of the Peace. Clark was then committed to York jail there to be held in custody until discharged by due process of law.

At the next session of the Superior Court of Judicature, Court of Assize and General Gaol Delivery held at York the 21st of June 1757, the jurors upon oath presented, "that John Clark late of a place called Pearson Town in said county of York, Laborer, not having a fear of God before his Eyes, but being seduced by the instigation of the Devil, did on the 13th day of March last between the hours of six and eight of the clock in the forenoon of his malice aforethought Kill and Murder James Wooster, laborer, of Pearsontown;" and his wife and daughter who had been confined in Falmouth jail since the crime were also indicted for "being present, aiding and encouraging Clark to commit the felony and murder." Upon the indictment the prisoners were at once "brot to the bar and arraigned and pleaded not guilty and for trial put themselves upon God and the Country." A jury was thereupon sworn to try the issue, Mr. George Hammond foreman, who having fully heard the evidence went out to consider thereof and returned with their verdicts and on their oath said that Jane Clark and Mary Clark were not guilty. It was therefore considered by the court that they go without delay. But as to John Clark the jury brought in a special verdict that "if the said Alexander Gray might lawfully by force enter the said John Clark's dwelling house to search for the goods without reading the Warrant to the said John Clark at the said house, then the Jury find the said John Clark guilty of murder otherwise they find him guilty of manslaughter only." The case was continued for advisement to be argued at Boston the next term. This postponement of judgement meant that Clark must lie in York Jail for a whole year as the next session of the court would not commence till June 20, 1758.

On the 18th of August two months after Clark's trial a Petition of Christopher Strout and others, Selectmen of the Town of Falmouth was received by the House of Representatives at Boston, "praying that they may be relieved in their charges of supporting two young children of one John Clark, an inhabitant of that part of York county, but not within the bounds of any township, who has for some time been imprisoned in her Majesty's Gaol at York on suspicion of murder."

Final action was not taken on this petition until March 18, 1758 when the House of Representatives, with the concurrence of the Council and approval of the Governor voted "that the maintenance of the children mentioned was properly a County charge and that the County of York should provide for the children until they could be bound out or taken care of by their parents." In accordance with these instructions, the Court of General Sessions of the Peace for York County ordered "that there be allowed and paid out of the County Treasury unto the Overseers of the Poor of the Town of Falmouth the sum of six pounds lawful money in full for boarding and keeping two children of John Clark's agreeable to an order of the Great and General Court of this province on file, and that the same to be in full for keeping and boarding said children from the 25th of March 1757 to the of 20th of October, last past.

The Superior Court of Judicature and Court of Assize was held at York the third Tuesday of June, 1758. In the records of the Clerk of Court we read under date of June 20th the following:

"At the last Term of Court one John Clark was indicted and tried for murder, and the Jury who were charged with the case brought in a special verdict which the Court chose to advise on until this term, and now directed the Sheriff to bring the said Clark into Court to hear their judgment upon the said verdict, upon which the Sheriff informed the Court that although he had used great precaution to secure the said Clark in gaol, he had found means to make his escape, and has not since been heard of."

James Wooster, the victim of Clark's homicidal act, was the great grandson of Rev. William Wooster of Salisbury, Mass., and brother of Timothy and William Wooster, early settlers of Falmouth. He was born Sept. 15, 1712 the son of Francis and Mary (Cheney) Wooster of Bradford, Mass. He was admitted to full communion in the First Church of Falmouth (Portland) May 30, 1736; married Feb. 26, 1740, a widow, Patience Low, the daughter of James Mills who is said to have built the second or third house on Falmouth Neck. Patience Wooster, after the death of her husband, married Dennis Larry of Gorham. The late Mrs. Phebe C. Dole, wife of Rev. Samuel T. Dole of South Windham was her great granddaughter.

— WILLARD W. WOODMAN. Peabody, Massachusetts, March 8, 1910.

[the newspaper clipping of this story was not dated nor the publication identified]

Accidental Shooting

Saturday forenoon, Clinton Noyes and Leo Clay of this town went out deer hunting on Standish plains. They had only been there a short time when two deer were sighted only about a hundred yards distant. Noyes was carrying a rifle and Clay a shot gun heavily loaded with buckshot. Both men drew at once and Clay in his excitement discharged his shot gun almost in direct range of Noyes. One shot struck Noyes in the arm, three in his shoulder and two in the thigh below the groin. Noyes suffered a good deal of pain from his wounds but his companion managed finally to get him where a physician could be called. Upon extracting the shot it was found that one of them had lodged within a few inches of the femoral artery, thus narrowly escaping inflicting a fatal injury.

— **Portland Daily Press, October 14, 1901**

Disorderly

Though yesterday was civil day in the municipal court, Recorder Wheldan tried the case of Lewis W. Jones of Standish. Jones is the man who was brought to the Station late Monday night by Constable Willard F. Cram of Standish, who arrested him for intoxication and disturbance. Jones gave considerable trouble before arrested and while being taken to the city. He pleaded guilty and was fined $3 and costs.

— **Portland Daily Press, August 20, 1902**

Missing

Strange Disappearance of Aged Man.
Daniel Johnson of Gorham Lost.
Drove to Sebago Lake Station Thursday.
Neither He Nor Team Seen Since Then.
Fears That He Has Become Temporarily Insane.

Daniel Johnson, a farmer aged 73 years, living In Gorham about two miles from the Sebago Lake station, has disappeared in a most unaccountable manner and since 12 o'clock Thursday night not a trace has been found of him.

Thursday evening, Mr. Johnson left his home to drive to the Sebago Lake station Mr. and Mrs. Clarence Bradbury who desired to take the train leaving that place at 7 o'clock for Portland. He did not return home and his whereabouts are a mystery. The strange part of it is that the team, which is a particularly conspicuous one, has not been seen either, though a rig resembling the one that Mr. Johnson was driving was seen at East Baldwin at Sebago Lake station and near White Rock in Gorham at different times during the night.

Mr. Johnson lives on his farm in Gorham with his wife and his granddaughter, Miss Lottie Johnson, who had made her home with the old folks since last spring. Thursday afternoon, the young lady was married to Mr. William Sanborn, and after the wedding the old gentleman took Mr. and Mrs. Bradbury, who were guests at the wedding, to the station as has been stated. Of course, no one took any particular notice of him as he drove away but as it grew late and he did not return the waiting folks at home became alarmed and finally notified some of the neighbors. Search was at once instituted for the missing man and it has continued without let up to the present time but without result.

Mr. Johnson had his little dog with him when he went away and the animal returned to the house at about 11 o'clock. A lap robe which has been fully identified as belonging to him was picked up about a quarter of a mile from Sebago Lake village on the road to East Baldwin and several people at the latter place say that a team answering to the description of Mr. Johnson's was seen there about 9 o'clock. The circumstance is particularly remembered by one or two from the fact that they heard a dog whine in the wagon. The team drove rather aimlessly about the place and then disappeared. Mr. Ralph Shaw of Sebago Lake says that he saw a team looking like the missing one drive up to the depot at 11 o'clock, two hours later than the time the team was seen at East Baldwin. An hour later, Mr. Van Carle, who lives a mile from White Rock, says he saw a team which he is very sure was Mr. Johnson's. The road upon which Mr. Van Carle lives is not the one the missing man would have taken to go home.

Mr. Johnson drove a white horse weighing about 900 pounds

and harnessed to a two seated beach wagon. A more conspicuous rig than this can hardly be imagined and yet despite the fact that strict search has been made in all the country about Sebago Lake no one has been found who has seen the team or man since he passed Mr. Van Carle's house at midnight and there may be a slight doubt of course whether even he saw him.

The only reasonable theory that has been suggested in connection with the case is that the old gentleman is suffering from aberration of the mind and is driving somewhere aimlessly about the Country or has been taken care of at some farm house on an out of the way road.

— **Portland Daily Press, September, 27, 1902**

Missing Man

Mr. Freeman Paine of Standish village has been missing since early in the morning of last Thursday. He then left his home and was seen afterward near "Dow's Corner." He has been much disturbed lately in his mind and there are indications that his brain had become enfeebled and disordered. It is feared that he has wandered into the deep woods, and becoming exhausted had been overcome by the severity of the weather and possibly he perished. Scouting parties have been diligently searching for him since Thursday but so far he has not been found.

— **Portland Daily Press, April, 28, 1890**

Fire at Standish

Village Sustained a $10,000 Loss Yesterday Morning.

The establishment of Henry B. Hartford, including a general store, dwelling house, stable, carriage house, post office, sale workshop, and printing office at Standish Corner, was destroyed by fire at an early hour this morning, entailing a loss that must exceed $10,000, and upon which there was an insurance approximating $6,000.

The buildings visited by the fire occupied a square of land in the center of the little village of Standish, covering as they did nearly a half-acre of land. The fire was discovered at 4:45 this morning by Mrs. J. E. Coombs, who occupied a tenement in the building. She hastened to arouse Mr. Hartford, and in a few moments the village was aroused by the cry of fire and the ringing of the church bells. There is no fire company organized in Standish, but the people turned out in large numbers and active work was done both in saving the buildings and their contents.

It soon became evident there was no hope of saving the buildings themselves, and the attention of the impromptu fire brigade was turned to the saving of buildings nearby.

Some tin force pumps proved of valuable assistance in preventing the spread of the flames.

The furniture was removed from the residence of Mr. Cressey, living nearby, and from the hotel, but they were both saved.

Mr. Hartford had recently hired a Mrs. Kennedy from Bristol, Conn., as his housekeeper. She has been there but three weeks, and quite a number of her personal belongings were destroyed, upon which she had no insurance.

Toward the northeast from the dwelling was the country store and post office. This store was exceptionally well stocked. Some goods were gotten out, but only in small quantities. The stock of goods must have been worth several thousand dollars.

Still further toward the northeast was the carriage house, from which seven or eight carriages were taken in safety. The stable, which was next in the line toward Sebago Lake village, was also burned, but the horses and other live inmates of the building were saved. There was only a small amount of hay destroyed.

The post office was kept in the store. It was in special charge of Mrs. Morrison, assistant postmaster. All the mail was taken out, as well as the books and papers belonging to the government, and the stock of stamped envelopes and wrappers.

A package of money which Mrs. Morrison took out, containing $150 or $200, was mislaid and probably lost.

In the southwesterly direction from the main dwelling on the road toward South Standish, was the sale workshop of Sawyer & Gray. Some of the machines were taken out of this building in safety, but most of the work in process of manufacture was destroyed. Mr. Gray reckons that his loss will reach $600 to $700. There was $1,800 worth of work from Boston houses. These were insured. About $75 worth of work from Lewis, Hall & Co., Portland, had no insurance on it.

The printing office, which was under Mrs. Coombs's dwelling, was the property of Harry B. Hartford, Jr. Not much was removed. Among the goods lost was a new press costing $500. There was no insurance.

The fire broke out near where the long funnel leading from the stove in the store enters a brick chimney. There was a wood fire in this stove Sunday and the only explanation that could be given was that the soot in the funnel caught fire and mulled along through the night finally igniting the woodwork through which the funnel passed.

About 15 people are thrown out of employment, besides those who did outside work for the sale work firm.

— Portland Daily Press, October 28, 1902

This photo of the Henry Hartford home, store and coat shop survived the 1902 fire. The building sat on the corner of Northeast road (route 35) and Ossipee Trail East (route 25), across from the house of Charles Tompson.

Was Drowned

Portland Man Probably Lost His Life at Sebago Lake.
HIS BOAT AND HAT FOUND.
Was Charles E. Libby,
Clerk in Rumford Falls R. R. Office.

Charles E. Libby, a clerk employed in the office of the Portland and Rumford Falls railroad in this city is missing, and has without doubt been drowned at Sebago Lake. Mr. Libby has resided for the past five years with his family at Oak Hill, Scarborough and has this summer been building himself a cottage at Sebago lake on Indian island. He owned a small motor boat on the lake and Saturday morning he went up on the first train and went over to the island in his launch. He had a boy with him and sent the boat back by him and saying that he would return that night in time to take the last train to Portland, in a punt that he had at the island.

He did not to do so and the next morning his folks telephoned to the lake to learn what had happened to him as he did not return as he was expected to do so. This inquiry resulted in a search being made and it was found that he had left the Island with the punt as he had planned to do so. There were some people who said that they saw him pass the gate house in his row boat about 6:30. This is the last so far as known that has been seen of him. Later an oar was found on the side of the lake next to the railroad and a little above the station.

Further search resulted in the finding of the boat itself which was on the shore between the gate house and the lake station. Nearby the boat was the missing man's hat. His card was found in it and the identification was complete.

The punt was a double ender affair: with the row locks in outriggers and one of these was broken! It is thought probable that when the row lock broke Mr. Libby fell overboard and was drowned. The body has not, however, been found.

Mr. Libby was the rating clerk in the office of the Portland and Rumford Falls railroad, and was one of the most valued men in the office. He was married and lived at Oak Hill, where he has resided for the past five years. His father, Richard Libby, and mother lived in one part of the house and his family in the other. Mr. Libby's wife was before her marriage Miss Eloise Milliken of Scarboro, a daughter of Melville Milliken. They have two little boys, one Richard, who was four years old last March, and another Robert, who was a year old in March. He also has a sister, Mrs. Joseph Henley, of Everett, Mass.

Mr. Libby was a member of Nonesuch lodge, Knights of Pythias, and one of its past chancellors.

— Portland Daily Press, August 18, 1903

Theodore Perry's Death

The coroner's jury in the case of Theodore Perry, who died as the result of injuries received in a recent railway accident at Sebago lake, yesterday returned a verdict in which they say that Theodore Perry of Standish, Me., came to his death at said Portland, the 22d day of October A. D., 1903, the result of an internal injury in the form of a rupture of the intestines received while in the discharge of his duties as brakeman an upon the caboose of freight train number 173, owned and operated by the Maine Central Railroad company, the said injury being inflicted by a blow upon the stomach caused by his being thrown from the top of said caboose upon the car in front and from thence to the ground, at said Standish, on the 20th day of October A. D. 1903

— **Portland Daily Press, October 27, 1903**

A Woman Fined for Trespass

Some Standish people gathered in the Municipal court Wednesday morning to listen to the trial of the complaint of trespass brought by William A. Hasty against Mrs. Mattie Weeks, the wife of Orlando Weeks. It seems that Hasty had some choice apples and he thought Mrs. Weeks went into his orchard and took them. So, he brought the trespass complaint and alleged that the fruit taken was worth a dollar. Mrs. Weeks was fined $10 and costs and paid.

— **Portland Daily Press, October 29, 1903**

Fatal Occurrence in Thorndike

On the morning of the 17th inst. Mrs. Eunice Philbrick, the widow of Gideon Philbrick, was so badly burnt by her clothes taking fire that she died the same evening. It is supposed that her clothes caught by her reaching up in front of the fire. There was no one in the room at the time, and she was completely wrapt in flames when her screams brought to her aid the inmates of the house. Her husband and herself emigrated from the town of Standish about the year 1800, and were among the first settlers of the town. When in the vigor of life, she was one of the most resolute and enterprising women of the pioneers. Her age was 87 years.

— **Republican Journal, February, 2, 1860**

Bronchotomy

Tbc operation of Bronchotomy was successfully performed in Standish, about three weeks since, by Dr. Cyrus Jordan, of Limington, on a child of Mr. David Chase, aged fourteen months, who had swallowed a piece of an acorn, which remained in its windpipe three hours-—during which time the child was in the greatest distress—respiration having become nearly extinct before the arrival of the physician.

— **Daily Eastern Argus, March 13, 1832**

Standish Farm Hand Arrested

Arthur Lane of Cornish Charged With Murder of Olive Broad

Case Against Prisoner Depends Almost Entirely on the Statement of Two Little Girls After eight months of investigation and search on the part of the officers of York county and detectives employed by the attorney general without enough evidence being obtained to warrant an arrest for the murder of Miss Olive H. Broad of Cornish. State Detective A. P. Bassett of Norway was employed by some of the friends and relatives of Miss Broad with the result that an arrest was made early yesterday on evidence obtained by Mr. Basssett.

The man under arrest and charged with the murder is Arthur S. Lane who was taken into custody before six o'clock yesterday morning at the farm of William Harmon in the town of Standish. Deputy Sheriff James C. Ayer of Cornish accompanied the state detective when the arrest was made on a warrant sworn out by the Methodist minister of Cornish, Rev. Charles H. Young. Late yesterday afternoon, Lane was arraigned before Trial Justice William B. Randall and at the request of the attorney for York county, George H. Emery, the case was continued until Friday, May 29, at 10 o'clock. Lane pleaded not guilty to the charge and asked the county attorney to have Edwin L. Poor of Standish notified of the arrest and asked to serve as his Counsel. Deputy Sheriff Ayer took Lane to Saco jail last night where he will remain until the hearing takes place.

The arrest of Lane came as a surprise to the people of Cornish or at least to the most of them and also to the county officials of York. Though eight months have passed since the body of Olive H. Broad was found in the wood road a short distance from the travelled highway leading from the Cornish station to the village and no person has been arrested whom the evidence would warrant being held for the crime, the officials of York have not been idle. Every clue that was forthcoming was run to earth, the most experienced men in the state have worked on the case and still the public could see nothing being accomplished. In fact, the officials were up against a proposition which seemed inexplicable and though every tramp theory and all other theories were run to the ground little was obtained.

There were some people in the town of Cornish who thought they had reason to suspect someone and tales of the wildest description have been the gossip of the countryside for months. But though these stories were all investigated, the linger of suspicion did not seem to point conclusively toward any one, or if it did designate any person there was not enough tangible material to warrant action by the officers of the law.

Things were in this shape when some of Miss Broad's relatives heard stories that interested them and they immediately took matters into their own hands. The result was that State Detective A. P. Bassett of Norway, a deputy sheriff of Oxford county, who will be remembered in Portland as the man who was the chief witness against Charles S. Swett when that hotel was raided for liquor just before the expiration of Sheriff Dunn's administration, was employed to visit Cornish and look into matters along the lines designated by some of the Cornish people.

Mr. Bassett arrived on Wednesday and having a fishing rod with him told those who inquired that he had come up to Cornish to try trout streams. This was a very innocent disguise and it was immediately noised about the town that Mr. Bassett was a noted detective from some place and everyone knew why he had come and at whose request. It took Mr. Bassett but two days to ascertain what was thought to be needed to warrant an arrest being made and as the result of his efforts Arthur S. Lane, a farm hand who comes of a good family but who unfortunately for him, has had a very unsavory reputation about this region, is now in Saco jail under a charge of murder.

THE MURDER OF MISS BROAD

It will be remembered that Miss Olive H. Broad was murdered on the second day of the Cornish fair, Wednesday August 20th. 1902. She was a middle aged woman who had a little property which was looked after by her nephew, James W. Hill of Brownfield. On the day of the murder Miss Broad had taken the morning train and gone to Center Conway to see some friends. She had little money with her, not much over $3 anyway. Sometimes when she went to Brownfield she brought back with her more money than this, but as she tried to get $5 changed by the hotel man at Center Conway before taking the train back to Cornish and told the hotel man that was all the money she had and she did not like to bother the station agent to change the bill for her, the conclusion naturally was that on this day she had not over $5.70, the fare from Center Conway to Cornish being 70 cents.

The train which Miss Broad took back to Cornish arrived at the latter place about 4:08 p.m. Miss Broad left the station and started up the road to Cornish village, said to be a mile away but in reality not quite as far as this. She was seen leaving the station but never reached her little home in Cornish.

At nine o'clock on the morning of Thursday, August 21, Louis Cook and his wife, who lived beyond the woods, when on their way home through a little wood road found Miss Broad's body about 120 rods from the main highway. The woman had received a slight cut over her right eye from a club or something of this kind and there was a bullet hole behind the right ear. The bullet which penetrated the woman's brain had been fired from a twenty-two calibre revolver. The wounds had bled but little. The body had been dragged a little ways into the underbrush by the side of the wood rood where it was found. Miss Broad's pocket book was missing.

Louis Cook and his wife had been at work during the early part of the morning cutting the little tufts of hay by the roadside and were on their way home when they discovered the body. These two people were the first taken into custody and several tramps were the next people arrested. There was a great deal of talk at the time about a "red faced" tramp being wanted and the officers scoured the country for red faced tramps with pretty good success for they found that about every tramp had a red face. One after another, these tramps were discharged. having proved themselves innocent and it was at this time that the people of Cornish began to question one another as to whether it was not someone among their own people or those living in the region who had committed the murder.

THE CHARGE AGAINST LANE

Mr. Bassett was told some tales when he reached Cornish on Wednesday which he proceeded to run down. These tales that were circulated among the village people emanated from Edna and Gertrude Sanborn, so it is believed. These two girls are 11 and 10 years old respectively. They live on the "Plains" at Cornish and have but lately moved into the town. Their sister married Arthur H. Lane.

These little girls told Mr. Bassett and County Attorney Emery a very straight story and they stuck to all they told in spite all cross examination. They said that on Wednesday, August 20th, Arthur Lane and his brother Luther went to the Cornish fair on their bicycles. Arthur did not get back to his home until after midnight on that night. He then went away with his wife and was gone two days and returned to his father-in-law's house in Buxton. The next morning he burned his soft felt hat and tried to give his father-in-law, George Sanborn, a pair of trousers. The father-in-law said he didn't want them because they were covered with blood. Arthur told his father-in-law that these trousers had caused him trouble enough and he thought he would get rid of them and he did bury them in a sand heap by the side of the house.

The little girls said that they had heard the murder talked over in the house by Arthur and others and had heard George Sanborn accuse his son-in-law of shooting Miss Broad for five dollars. George Sanborn, the girl's father, and Arthur quarreled a great deal and whenever the old man got mad he accused Arthur of the murder.

Finally one day, the little girls dug up the trousers and say that they were stained as though by blood and then buried them again where Arthur had put them. The girls also told Mr. Bassett that

Arthur had at that time a revolver, a small revolver, they said, which he afterwards sold to some people living in Standish whom they did not know.

Detective Bassett then went to the house formerly occupied by Lane's father-in-law in Buxton and there in a sand heap by the side of the house dug out a pair of old trousers which the little girls said were the same that Arthur Lane had buried there. These trousers were stained above the knees in front and were also badly decayed; What had occasioned the stains could not be determined by Mr. Bassett but he thought they were blood stains and said he believed they came from the head of Olive Broad when she was dragged into the wood road by the murderer.

George Sanborn, Lane's father-in-law, died last November so that his testimony could not be had but the detective interviewed Mrs. Sanborn who now lives in Cornish and thought he had evidence sufficient to warrant Lane's arrest.

THE ARREST

The facts of the case were then put before Trial Justice Randall and he issued the warrant on the complaint of Rev. Charles H. Young, who had taken much interest in the case. Then Deputy Sheriff James C. Ayer was called into conference and told of the facts Mr. Bassett had obtained. Mr. Ayer said he was willing to serve the warrant but told Mr. Bassett and others that Lane's case had been investigated last Fall by County Attorney Emery and

Sheriff Miles and they had not seen fit to arrest him.

But In the end, Mr. Ayer and Mr. Bassett drove over to William Harmon's house In Standish. It was a long drive and they started at three o'clock in the morning and got to the house about six. Mrs. Lane, Arthur's wife, heard the noise of the team as it drove into the dooryard and met the men at the door. Mr. Bassett said he wanted to see Mr. Lane to get him to go to work for him. Lane was half-dressed and came to the door and the officer had then gotten inside. He saw Deputy Sheriff Ayer and said: "You want me for the Cornish murder?" The officers told him this was so. Mr. Ayer told a PRESS reporter that Lane said he knew right off what the officers wanted him for us soon as he saw Deputy Sheriff Ayer.

The man was nervous and did not cool down until he had been riding with the officers for some time. He told them his story then and to three or four people he told the same story afterwards with all its details and without any variation.

Lane's story as he related it to a PRESS reporter was as follows:

LANE'S STORY

"On Tuesday night before this Cornish murder I had a row with Sanborn, my father in law. It was over some flour. His wife wanted to borrow some flour from a new barrel which I had not opened and I wouldn't open it. This and other things started the row. I had been drinking and was a little hot. Arthur Guptill was there and made some talk and I tried to put him out of the house. My wife asked me to come home and we started to go. As we left the house, I heard my father-in-law say something and call me names. I went back and asked him if he was talking about me. He said he was and came at me with what I thought was a piece of board but what they say was the handle of a bicycle. He struck at me and I hit him in the breast and he fell down. They made a great fuss over it and Sanborn said he would have me arrested for assault.

"I didn't want to be arrested, so, the next morning, I took my bicycle and said I was going to Gorham to see my father and see if I couldn't get a job with him and go down there until this affair blew over. I thought the officers would not go down there to get me. The first stop I made was at Will Parker's house in Buxton where my brother was working. I got there about ten o'clock having left home about nine. This was on the morning of the first day of the Cornish fair the day Miss Broad was murdered.

"I staid at Parker's about half an hour. I did not see Parker then but saw my brother and Mrs. Parker. Then I went on to father's house in Buxton. My father was at Gorham at work in his shop or on some job. He is a carpenter. I got dinner there. Mrs. Sawyer, my father's housekeeper, an old lady, giving me the dinner. I then rode on to Gorham and got there about one o'clock. I went into a church there in which they were putting in a steel celling and there I saw Everett Elwell. I stayed there in the church until about three o'clock and went to South Gorham to the house of Freeman Moulton. I staid there until about four o'clock and then rode back to Gorham."

The reader will remember that Miss Broad was murdered somewhere about 4:15 o'clock on the afternoon when Lane says he was on the road between Gorham and South Gorham.

"I rode back to Gorham and was in the church there when they knocked off work at five o'clock. The last thing I did was to go to my father's shop and asked him for a job. He told me that he had nothing for me to do that would pay him to hire me for. So, I started back to Buxton. I got supper at my father's house about six o'clock and left about seven for home. I stopped at Will Parker's on the way back home and saw him and my brother George who, is now dead, and got home late. I don't know when for I went to bed without lighting a light.

"The next morning I was told by Arthur Guptill that the officers had a warrant for me and were looking for me so I thought I wouldn't stay about home. I took my wheel and rode to Cornish and got there about nine o'clock I guess."

This was on the day and about the time that Miss Broad's body was discovered.

"I thought I would look for a house to live in and would move up there. The other side of the covered bridge now an old house and nearby was man and a woman culling hay by the side of the road. The man told me his name was Cook."

This was the man and woman who discovered Miss Broad's body and the place where Lane met Cook and his was within a stone's throw of the scene of the murder. Yesterday, Cook corroborated Lane's statement about the meeting. Frank Milliken of Baldwin also says he met Lane at that time.

Lane continued his story as follows: "I asked Cook who owned the house and he told me that it belonged to Jim Ayer the deputy sheriff. I rode up to the village and they told me that Ayer was up to the fairgrounds. I went up there and staid around awhile on the outside but didn't go inside because I didn't want to spend the money for that little while and I thought Ayer would come out. Then someone told me there was a warrant out for my arrest and that the officer who had it had come up on the morning train after me."

The warrant of which Lane spoke was that which he believed would be issued because of the trouble with his father-in-law.

"I thought I wouldn't stay around there so I rode on towards Parsonsfield to John French's where I got dinner. French is a relative of my mother. I looked at some houses at Porter village and couldn't find what I wanted and so turned back to Cornish to see if I couldn't hire the house of Mr. Ayer. On the way back, I met Frank Emery who was driving by and he told me that they had discovered a horrible murder at Cornish. This was the first I had heard of the murder. Emery lives in Eppingham Falls.

"I got back home at Mattocks late at night and told my wife we had better get out as there was a warrant out for my assault on Sanborn, my father-in-law, and as I didn't have any money to pay a fine I thought the best thing to do was to sell out and go somewhere else. So, I sold out all my stuff and my wife and I started towards Brownfield on the railroad track that night getting there late at night and spending the day in the station.

Then we walked to Snow Village. N. H. where I hoped to get work. I couldn't get work there, so, after a few days when my money was gone, we walked home to my father's and staid there."

"What color were those trousers you gave your father-in-law?" asked the PRESS reporter of Lane.

"I did not give him any trousers last fall. A year ago, after I was burned out, I gave him a pair of trousers. I had no hats to burn up and never burned up a hat. I never owned a revolver either, as they say I did. I never liked guns und never went hunting in my life. It was too much like work.

"I can't see why these girls should tell any story like this about me. I never had any trouble with them and the trouble I had with old man Sanborn was long ago. I know of no one who is an enemy of mine but someone must have put those girls up to that story. It is all a lie. The story I have told you is the truth and I can prove it too."

THE PRISONER'S PAST LIFE

The prisoner told this story in a straightforward way that impressed all who heard it. He said that he had told the same story last fall to Sheriff Miles and Mr. Emery, the county attorney. It was said yesterday at Cornish that those two officials had investigated the story told by Lane at the time and had pursued this matter no further. According to Lane's story, he was between South Gorham and Gorham, twenty-two and a half miles from the scene of the murder at the time it occurred. If the witnesses he has named will corroborate his story it should not be a difficult thing for him to prove an alibi.

Lane has been mixed up in some wild scrapes, however, and has a rather unsavory reputation. In 1893, County Attorney Emery, then but recently admitted to the bar of York county, defended Lane in a case brought against him for killing a cow and a calf and wounding a horse in Baldwin. Lane was at Buxton Center and got on a hard cider drunk. He went into Baldwin and into a man's barn. In the morning or that night, he got onto the man's horse and rode him around the yard and when the animal would not go where he wanted him to be he stuck a knife into him. The animal was badly wounded but was not killed. Then Lane got onto the back of a cow and finally cut her throat and also killed a calf in the same way. For this act he was arrested and served 18 months in the Cumberland county jail.

Right after the death of Sheriff Pearson and before his successor was appointed, Lane got into a fight with his brother in Naples or somewhere in that region in which it was alleged axes figured prominently and it was said that Lane fired a charge of buckshot into his brother. Lane denied the story yesterday and said he had been drunk. There was a fight but it was badly exaggerated and no one was badly hurt. He was never arrested for the affair.

Lane is a youth of 22, his face tanned by the sun until it is of a copper hue. He has black hair and dark eyes and a sharp face with thin nose and prominent chin. He looks at first glance as though he had some Indian blood in his veins. He was poorly dressed and his hair was much longer than men usually like to wear it. He is not very prepossessing in appearance, and until one talks with him, his appearance is rather against him. But he talks readily, smiles frequently and yesterday was not at all nervous in his manner.

THE ARRAIGNMENT

He was arraigned at about six o'clock in the law office of Mr. Randall, the trial Justice. He pleaded not guilty and County Attorney Emery asked for a continuance of a week which was granted.

Lane said he wanted E O. Poor as his counsel and was told he could have him if he wanted him. County Attorney Emery refused to even suggest where the prisoner be kept until the time of the hearing. He said it was all a matter for the officers to decide. After a conference in which Mr. Bassett, the detective, suggested keeping the man in Cornish with a keeper to look after him. It was decided to take Lane to the Saco jail.

County Attorney Emery refused to be interviewed by a PRESS reporter as to what he thought of the case. He said: "'At this time I do not care to state what I think of this case. I shall get to the bottom of this evidence however."

It was rumored about the village of Cornish last night that now that Lane is under arrest some timid people might have evidence to give which before they did not dare to give to the officers. The little girls said that Lane had threatened to kill anyone who told the officers anything about what they might know about his connection with the murder case.

— **Portland Daily Press, May 23, 1903**

His Story True

Arthur Lane Can Establish a Perfect Alibi
ACCUSED OF CORNISH MURDER
Five Responsible Men Say He Was Elsewhere.

Buxton, May 23.—Substantial Citizens of Buxton and Gorham will be on hand In Cornish next Friday to defend the alibi set up by Arthur S. Lane, who is under arrest on a charge of the murder of Miss Olive H. Broad.

Lane formerly lived here, and though he has borne a rather unsavory reputation, and his townsmen have no great love or respect for him, they believe him innocent of the charge on which he is now held. Several residents will testify that they saw and talked with him here, more than 20 miles from Cornish, the very afternoon that Miss Broad was dragged into the Cornish woods, shot and robbed.

When Lane was suspected, shortly after the murder, the York county prosecuting officers at work on the case, came here and satisfied themselves that he was not the murderer. Today, a reporter who has been familiar with the developments of the murder investigation drove over the route which Lane claims to have ridden on a bicycle, August 20, the day of the murder, and located nine persons whose testimony ought to be of service to the prisoner. Four of them are not positive, in regard to the date, though their statements corroborate his in every other particular. Five persons, outside the family of the accused man, state positively that the day he visited Gorham and Buxton was August 20, the second day of the Cornish fair.

Perhaps the most important of these are George Cressey, William Parker, and the latter's two sons. Mr. Parker owns a large farm on the direct road from Baldwin to Groveville village, the road Lane claims to have ridden over on his brother's bicycle on the day in question. Mr. Parker says he knows it was the second day of the Cornish fair, for his two boys went to the fair that day and stayed so long that he worried about them. The younger one, made the 20-mile trip on his bicycle. "I was in front of my house about 7:15 that evening." Mr. Parker said, "and, I saw a man coming on a bicycle, from the direction of Groveville village. He spoke to me and I went out to see who it was. It was Arthur Lane. He dismounted and I asked him where he was going. He said that he was headed for his home in Baldwin. I told him I wouldn't ride his wheel to Baldwin for more that its value. He replied that he had come down from in Baldwin that morning. He told me about visiting Gorham village."

George Cressey, an honest appearing young farmer who lives a half mile from Parker's is positive about the date. He didn't see Lane, but Mr. Cressey had his initiatory degree In Saco Valley lodge of Odd Fellows, the night of Wednesday, August 20. He says he intended going to the lodge with Parker, but was a little late in reaching Parker's house. Parker was standing in front of the house, and when Cressey came along told him that Arthur Lane had just gone ahead on his bicycle. The lodge records show that Mr. Cressey was initiated August 20.

Ernest Parker saw Lane that morning bicycling toward Groveville, and the other Parker boy passed Lane on the Groveville road in the early evening headed toward Baldwin.

According to Lane's alibi, he was at Freedom A. Moulton's house in South Gorham, 22 miles from Cornish, about the time the killing of Miss Broad occurred. The reporter visited Moulton's today and interviewed two members of that household. Mr. Moulton formerly kept store in Groveville village. He said that he could recall everything about Lane's visit there except the date. His impression was that the Cornish fair was in progress, but he hadn't yet arrived at the point where he could positively recall the day of the month or week. Lane was there from 3pm until about 3:45pm. Mr. Moulton said he believed he would be able to clear his mind on the subject. He should do all in his power to do so, but he did not want to say what day it was.

Mr. Moulton's wife, though not at home when Lane called, is able to throw substantial light on the subject. She says she spent the last week of August in Boston, leaving Portland by boat, the night of Monday, the 25th, and returning home Labor day. She remembers that the Wednesday before her departure for Boston she and a neighbor went to Portland, shopping. She had seen some dry goods advertisements which attracted her attention and that prompted her to make the shopping trip. She bought a suit at J. R. Libby Co.'s and a hat at R. M. Lewsen's. When she returned home that evening her husband told her she had missed a call from Arthur Lane, and related conversation he had with Lane, that afternoon.

Everett Elwell. a carpenter of Groveville. who was employed in putting the steel ceiling in the Orthodox church in Gorham village, last August, says he remembers that Arthur Lane visited Gorham early one afternoon and was there again just before the crew quit work. The crew had been discussing the Cornish races, but Mr. Elwell said he cannot positively state what day of the month it was, or what day of the fair. When he passed the Lane homestead, on the way to Groveville, just before 6 o'clock, he saw Arthur Lane there with the wheel he had ridden in Gorham.

William H. Lane, father of the prisoner, is a prominent building contractor at Gorham and Buxton whose word, his townsmen declare, is as good as his bond. Mr. Lane expressed pleasure at the result of the interviews with the persons here mentioned, but was unable to add to the array of positive evidence in regard to the date of his son's visit to Gorham. "I remember he called on me and was about the village a part of the afternoon." said Mr. Lane. He asked me about work and told me where he had been. I have been trying to recall what day it was, but my memory doesn't help me in that particular. There is nothing I can fix the date by. My payroll shows that my crew was putting in the church ceiling in Gorham the week beginning the 18th. but that doesn't go very far toward fixing the date Arthur was here."

Mr. Lane says he believes the young man is innocent, but hopes he will not escape punishment if he is guilty of murder.

Mrs. Sawyer, the aged housekeeper at the Lane homestead, told the reporter about Arthur Lane taking dinner there at noon and supper about six o'clock, the day he came on his brother's wheel, but she is unable to definitely fix the time.

County Attorney Emery and Detective Bassett of Norway have been interviewing witnesses in preparation for Friday's hearing. It is believed here that the county attorney is personally convinced, as he was last fall, that Lane is not the murderer and that after the testimony in support of the alibi has been heard there will be nothing to do but discharge the prisoner.

Arthur Lane's wife and his attorney, Lawyer Poor of Sebago, visited Gorham today. She said she believes her husband innocent. She remembers that he left home, August 20, about 9 o'clock in the morning, and she saw him go in the direction of Buxton. It was about 9:30 when he returned that night. He had a pair of shoes that his father had given him in Groveville.

Mrs. Lane says that the stories told by her little sisters about Arthur burying a pair of trousers are lies, probably inspired by someone prejudiced against him. He had only one pair of trousers in August.

Asked if the children have been on good terms with her husband she replied: "Mother hates Arthur and has prejudiced the children against him."

— **Portland Daily Press, May 25, 1903**

Arthur Lane's Alibi

Lawyer Deering Finds Witnesses Who Are Positive.

Biddeford, May 27.—John Percy Deering, counsel for Arthur S. Lane of West Buxton, accused of the murder of Miss Olive Broad of Cornish, returned today from Gorham, where he has been investigating the story told by his client, relative to his whereabouts on the day of the murder. He went over the territory yesterday reported to have been traversed by Lane on the day of the murder, and found that there are several persons who are able to fix with certainty the date, August 20, the day of the murder, as being the time they saw Lane in Gorham and vicinity. There are a number of others who are reasonably sure of the day, but are not able to fix it so positively.

Lawyer Deering will make another trip to Gorham for additional evidence before the hearing.

A Cornish man who was in town today says that Detective Bassett is putting lots of work into the case, and will have some important witnesses testify at the hearing.

— Portland Daily Press May 28, 1903

Charged with Murder

**Evidence Against Arthur Lane Accused
of Killing Olive Broad
SANBORN GIRLS A DISAPPOINTMENT
A Promised Sensation Which Did Not Materialize
Adjournment to Tuesday.**

Cornish, May 29 - The question of whether there is evidence enough against Arthur S. Lane, the Standish farm hand, to warrant his being held for the grand Jury of the September term of the York county Supreme court has not yet been settled. Today, Trial Justice William B. Randall of Cornish listened seven hours, in a crowded public hall, to testimony introduced in behalf of the state, and at the conclusion of the afternoon session 10 of the state's witnesses had not been examined. A dozen or more witnesses summoned by the defense in support of Lane's alibi stood around all day with no prospect of their side of the case being reached before next week. The hearing was continued until Tuesday.

The state's case, so far as it was presented today, and the bulk of the material testimony, fell short of what was anticipated, in view of statements previously made by several of the chief witnesses. The testimony of the two little Sanborn girls, sisters-in-law of Lane, whose stories about his burying a pair of blood-stained trousers were the groundwork of the prosecution of Lane, was especially disappointing. They made conflicting statements, contradicted each other and either denied or couldn't remember having told Detective Bassett and the York county officers "certain stories" which were to have been introduced on behalf of the state.

Detective A. F. Bassett of Norway, who made the arrest, was questioned at great length in regard to the reason of his coming into York county, seven months after the murder, and working up the case without the knowledge of the authorities here. He said he came at the request of relatives and friends of Miss Olive H. Broad, the murdered woman. In response to the inquiries of attorneys on both sides of the case, he said that his invitation was a letter from Rev. Charles H. Young, the Methodist pastor in Cornish. which stated that the relatives and friends of Miss Broad wanted detective assistance.

It had been anticipated, on the strength of certain broad hints thrown out during the week, that at this hearing a sensation would be sprung. This promised sensation did not materialize today, but the defending attorneys say it will surely come Tuesday.

It was a gala day for Cornish, this first day of the Lane hearing. The village streets were lined with teams and the Smith & Warren Company's public hall in the top story of a business block, was crammed almost to suffocation all day. There were seats enough for the state's witnesses, but defending witnesses had to shift for themselves. Prominent citizens of Cornish sat on the little stage, beside the trial Justice. The few settees on the floor were held down all day, some of their occupants eating picnic dinners in the hall, in preference to running the risk of losing their seats. Of the 500 persons attending the hearing, nearly 400 stood, and seemed glad of the chance.

County Attorney George L. Emery of Biddeford conducted the prosecution. At his beck and call were Sheriff Fogg, Deputies Miles of Saco and Ayer of Cornish and Detective Bassett.

The prisoner was defended by John P. Deering of Saco and E. A Poor of Sebago, who look turns cross examining state witnesses. The Methodist minister had a seat well up front, and attentively watched proceedings.

PROVED THE CRIME

The county attorney, in his opening, after briefly outlining the state's case, said the testimony would be put in for whatever it was worth. It was well known, he said, that the defense would be an alibi. If the alibi is proven to the satisfaction of any reasonable man. It would be the duty of the magistrate to discharge the prisoner; but if the alibi is not absolutely proven the respondent should be held.

First the county attorney introduced evidence to prove that a murder was committed, and went deeply into the movements of

Miss Broad Wednesday, August 20 and the finding of her dead body in a clearing off the woods road, half way between the station and village, the next morning.

Mrs. Ann L. Webb, whose family occupied the tenement adjoining that of Miss Broad, was first questioned in regard to Miss Broad's departure for Conway. Then Clinton Cole, proprietor of the Center house at Conway, and his daughter, May Cole, were examined. Mr. Cole changed a $5 bill for Miss Broad, just before she left his store, so it is practically certain that her pocketbook, missing when her body was found, contained less than that amount, she having spent 10 cents for a railroad ticket to Cornish.

Mrs. Flora A. Miles of West Baldwin drove by Miss Broad, about 4:18, on the road, a few rods from where the murder was committed. Joseph H. Bentoh, about 4:18, heard two pistol shots, the sound coming from the direction of the woods where the murder occurred. Lewis Cook and wife met Arthur Lane on the station road, Thursday morning, a few minutes before the body was found. This Lane admitted in his talk with the reporters the day of his arrest, but he explained that he was going to the Cornish fair.

Deputy Sheriff Ayer of Cornish described the position and condition of the body, and Dr. William H. Smith and Dr. Samuel G. Sawyer testified in relation to the post mortem. There was a bruise on the right side of her forehead, and two bullet wounds, made by a 22-calibre cartridge, were found, either one of which might have been sufficient to cause death.

AFTERNOON TESTIMONY

Henry J. Small, horseman, who was at the fair August 20, said he was cooling out a stallion during the races and saw a man whom he believed was the respondent "I think he is the man; I won't be positive," the witness said. The man in question was accompanied by an older man. They drove in a buggy on to the grounds and provoked witness by their careless driving.

Cross-examined by Mr. Deering, witness said Nelson Sargent was with him. Their horse was sorrel and their vehicle a top buggy. The two men in the buggy appeared to be selling liquor. From that day until last Friday, witness said he never again saw Lane.

A CHILD WITNESS

The name of Gertrude Sanborn was called and a pretty little dark-complexioned girl, with black eyes and black hair, came to the chair reserved for witnesses. She blushingly concealed beneath her short skirts a pair of shoes considerably the worse for wear. She said she is 11 years of age. Mr. Deering wanted to ascertain if she realized the nature of an oath. The county attorney questioned her briefly and expressed the opinion that she was qualified to testify. The court thought so too.

The little witness scarcely raised her eyes in making her replies. She said that last August her folks were living in Baldwin and Arthur Lane, her brother-in-law, was there. Up to that time she and Arthur had been good friends: he had always been good to her, never whipped her. She said that Arther Lane wasn't there; she couldn't recall that Arthur said he was going to the Cornish Fair: she couldn't remember having made such a statement to the county attorney.

The county attorney found occasion to criticize the mother of the witness. Mrs. Sanborn sat facing the child and by nod and gesture to prompt her. The mother, being threatened with removal from the court room if she persisted, promised to keep still.

Witness was then questioned in regard to the alleged sudden disappearance of Arthur Lane's hat. Her recollection on that point was rather hazy. An old, dirty light felt hat was shown her and she said it was the hat Arthur wore to Cornish. She said the next day he went away again and when he came home had a new hat on. He sold a barrel of flour and his furniture to William Nason.

"Has Arthur ever told you not to tell what you are testifying today?" the county attorney asked.

The witness did not reply. The county attorney assured her that no harm could come to her if she told the truth. Then he asked:

"Has Arthur ever threatened you if you told anything about him?"

"No he hasn't," the witness replied.

A portion of her statement made to the county attorney last week was read from the stenographer's transcription. The child admitted she made such a statement.

"Do you mean for me to understand then, that you lied to me when you told me in Lawyer Randall's office that Arthur threatened you?" the county attorney asked.

The child smiled behind her clinched hands, but did not reply. She was asked to describe the trousers Arthur wore last August. She said they had a light stripe. She thought she would recognize them if she should see them again. The garment which Detective Bassett dug up in the old Lane house on Smut street, East Baldwin, was shown her. "Those are Arthur's pants." she said. She said Arthur gave them to her papa, who didn't wear them but put them in the window where the glass was broken. She saw a red stain on them that she thought looked like blood. She saw Arthur bury the trousers when he banked the house. She and her sister later dug up the trousers to see if there was any blood on them.

The county attorney renewed and pressed his question about her alleged fear of Arthur Lane. The little girl began to cry. Again the county attorney assured her that she had nothing to fear. Through her tears, in response to his repeated questions, she said she was afraid of Arthur.

FIRST TOLD MRS WEBB

"To whom did you first tell this story, Gertrude?" Mr. Deering asked in beginning his cross examination.

"I told it to Mrs. Webb," the witness replied.

"'Who is Mrs. Webb?"

"That lady back there." The witness pointed to the first witness in the hearing.

"How did you happen to tell her about it?"

"She asked me."

"You didn't say anything to her until she asked you?"

"You were not afraid of Arthur last August, were you?"

"No."

"You are not afraid of him today, are you?"

"No."

"With whom else have you talked about this matter?"

"With Mr. Young, the minister."

"Have you talked with Mrs. Webb more than once about it?"

"Yes sir."

"Talked with her every time you called at her house?"

"Yesir."

"Did you tell your story to Mr. Bassett?"

"Yesir."

"Did he come to your house and ask you about it?"

"No. he was at the minister's."

Did you tell him you were afraid of Arthur?"

"No."

"When was the first time you were afraid of Arthur?"

"Today."

"Did you tell your story to Mrs. Webb the first time you called at her house?"   ...   .

"Yes sir."

"How did you happen to go to her house?"

"She asked Edna and me to come down."

"And you told her the story about the trousers?"

"Yes."

"When did you next tell the story and to whom?

"We told it to the minister. We were at Mrs. Webb's and the minister was there. She asked us to tell him about the pants and we did."

Mr. Deering brought out the trousers, showed them to the little witness and asked her if she remembered about her father having trouble with Arthur, last August. She said she did remember it. Her father didn't drink and wouldn't have liquor around. Arthur had been drinking and they fought. This fight was before the Cornish murder.

"Who had on those trousers when Arthur and your papa had the fight?" the defending attorney asked, holding up the garment.

"Papa did," was the reply.

"You are sure?"

"Yes."

"Was it before then that Arthur gave the trousers to your papa?"

"Yes."

"Did you tell Mrs. Webb the first time you called at her house, that you were afraid of Arthur?"

"NO."

"Did you tell the minister you were afraid of Arthur."

"NO"

"And you are not, are you?"

"No, I'm not."

ANOTHER CHILD

Edna Sanborn, 14 years of age, a sister of Gertrude, was next examined. She seemed to possess the average intelligence for a person of her age and her answers were more prompt, but her testimony was less strong than her statements to the officers before the trial, and in some material particulars conflicting.

She said she had never seen any bloodstains on the trousers and never heard any talk about blood on them, but she and Gertrude tried to dig up the garment to find out if there was blood on it.

This witness said she also told Mrs. Webb about the trousers and afterwards told the story to the minister and Detective Bassett. The county attorney asked her why she didn't mention the trousers to the officers who were hunting last fall for information. She did not reply, though the question was twice repeated.

"Did Arthur ever threaten you?" she was asked.

"No."

"Why not?"

"Papa told us not to tell."

"Did Arthur ever tell you he would fix you if you told?"

"No."

"Do you remember asking me, a week ago today, if Arthur Lane was coming into Mr. Randall's office, and that when I said he was coming in you ran out?"

"No, I don't remember."

The witness did not agree with her sister's identification of the hat in the case. It was a different colored hat that Arthur wore when he left home in the direction of Cornish, she said.

Cross examined by Mr. Poor, the witness said the trousers in the case her father wore two or three days after Arthur gave them to him. Then her father put them in the window and they remained there about two months. She didn't know who buried them.

Mr. Poor tried to find out why she dug up the trousers, but she was unable to explain. Gertie proposed digging them up, she said. They were frozen down, and after tearing the trousers in trying to dig them up the girls buried them again.

Witness related conversations she had with Mrs. Webb and the minister and detective about the trousers. She had visited Mrs. Webb's house a number of times. She and Gertrude were at the ministers last evening.

The county attorney explained that he requested the minister to talk with the children last evening.

"All right." said Mr. Poor. "If it was at your request. But thus far in this hearing the evidence disclosed seems to be a case of Webb and Young, and Young and Webb. I wanted to find out what the children were doing at the minister's last evening."

The county attorney asked:

"Have you told Mr. Bassett that your sister Clara wanted you to lie about this case?"

"I don't think I said that," the witness replied.

"Don't you know whether you did?"'

"I said to him that Clara didn't like it very well because I had told him about that."

"Are you positive you didn't tell him that Clara wanted you to lie here today?"

"I am positive."

UNSATISFACTORY WITNESSES

John Sanborn and his wife didn't pan out as well as the prosecuting attorney had hoped. They admitted that they were not positive about certain statements they made to him at their home a few days ago. The wife proved to be a fair witness for the defense. She said she witnessed the fight between Arthur and his father-in-law, and that the father-in-law then had on the trousers which was today exhibited in the case.

Albert E. Cressey of Groveville, Buxton, testified that Charles Lane, a brother of the respondent, had a revolver last July. The county attorney said Charles Lane and Arthur were in camp together last August.

It was brought out in cross examination that Charles Lane at this time was working away from home; witness didn't know whether the revolver belonged to Charles Lane or was borrowed.

Herman Sanborn of Hiram was another state witness whose statement under oath did not agree with his alleged previous statement to an officer. Witness had told about hearing two pistol shots. He wasn't sure whether the shots were from a revolver or small rifle. A boy down on Smut street has a 22 calibre rifle. Witness never saw either of the Lane boys have a firearm.

DETECTIVE BASSETT UNDER FIRE

Albert P. Bassett, the Norway state detective who worked up the case against Lane and arrested him, was next called. He said he has been a deputy sheriff 20 years, a coroner, fish and game warden, and about ten years a state detective. He came here, he said, at the request of relatives and friends of Miss Broad, the murdered woman. Being questioned further, witness said he came in response to a letter from Mr. Young the Methodist pastor, the letter stating that it was written at the request of relatives and friends of Miss Broad, but named no one. Witness come to Cornish May 10, called on the minister, and that evening interviewed the two Sanborn children.

As a result of that conversation, he and the minister drove to East Baldwin. Accompanying them was a carriage containing Mrs. Walter Webb and her cousin. Miss Myrtle Files, and the two Sanborn children. The youngest Sanborn girl pointed out where the trousers were buried, in the banking of the old Lane house. He dug up the trousers, and handed them over to the keeping of the minister. The warrant was sworn out by the minister, who volunteered to be complainant. Before the warrant was issued by Trial Justice Randall, the little Sanborn girls were called in and questioned.

The county attorney objected to the witness constantly referring to a note book before testifying. The detective put the note book in his pocket and continued his testimony without further reference to it. He said that when he first saw Lane, at Mr. Harmon's farm in Standish, early last Friday morning, Lane said: In response to a "Good morning" greeting, "You are an officer, and are after me for killing that lady up to Cornish. This is just what I expected."

Cross-examined by Lawyer Poor, Detective Bassett admitted that he had examined only two witnesses, the little Sanborn girls, when the warrant was issued; that the Methodist minister volunteered to sign the warrant as complainant. The minister and detective together drove to the Lane house where the old trousers were dug up. Mr. Walter Webb and her cousin, Mrs. Myrtie Files accompanied the little Sanborn girls on that drive and were present at the digging up of the trousers.

Mr. Poor asked Detective Bassett who would pay his bills. The county attorney objected and said the defense had thus far failed to connect anyone with an illegal or unfair motive in the prosecution of case. The question was excluded.

The hearing at 5:30 was adjourned until Tuesday, and Lane was taken across county to Alfred, for safe keeping until that day.

THOUGHT THEY SAW LANE

Ivory A. Lane, a Buxton farmer, who hadn't seen Arthur Lane before in four years, thought he saw him pass in the Cornish fairgrounds, the second day of the fair, about noon, August 20. He wasn't positive.

— Portland Daily Press, May 30, 1903

Evidence All In

Arguments Today In the Cornish Murder Case
A STRONG ALIBI FOR LANE
The Minister Shut Off In His Story of Investigation

Cornish. June 2.—Arthur S. Lane's alibi in the Cornish murder case was presented in detail to Trial Justice William B. Randall today, in the public hall where for two days young Lane has faced his accusers.

His story, recited in his cool, convincing manner, was substantially as he related it to the reporters here the day of his arraignment, ten days ago. The witnesses in Buxton and Gorham whose statements in support of his alibi were published last week were all on hand to give their testimony, and several more had been hunted up by the defending attorneys. Six of these witnesses stated positively that they saw Lane more than 20 miles from Cornish the afternoon of the murder. Another witness talked with Lane the afternoon of his visit in Gorham village but was unable to fix the time more definitely than to state that it was during the week of the Cornish fair. Two more witnesses, residents of East Baldwin, said they saw Lane start on a wheel toward

Gorham, the morning of August 20.

Lane was hardly recognized by his acquaintances when he came into the presence of the magistrate, this morning. He had undergone a striking change since he was taken to the Alfred jail, Friday night. He had on a new suit of clothes, a pair of new tan shoes, was cleanly shaven and had parted company with his verdant crop of black hair. He looked as well as anyone in the hall, and seemed quite as much at ease as those who gazed at him all day. His father had taken pity on the boy's condition and fitted him out in the attractive manner described.

The Methodist pastor Rev. Charles H. Young, occupied the seat of inquiry in the center of the arena for a half hour at the beginning of the forenoon session. He wasn't allowed to tell all he wanted to about the case. When quizzed by Lawyer Deering, in cross- examination, about his connection with the case, the pastor appealed to the court and asked that he be allowed to tell in his own way all the facts relating to his connection with it. He explained that he made this request in view of the fact that so many of his people were present. The court and the county attorney instructed the witness that he must simply answer the questions addressed to him.

He admitted that he invited Detective Bassett to come here and pursue the investigation. Then the witness was questioned in relation to the unearthing of the old trousers that had been buried in the banking of the house on Smut street, East Baldwin, where Lane lived in August. The two little Sanborn girls pointed to the spot where they were to dig, and the detective did the digging with a spade which the minister had procured for him. Witness said he noticed near one knee some stains that they thought might be bloodstains. He took charge of the trousers, locked them in his secretary, and kept them there until they were delivered to the sheriff.

Mr. Deering took up the old trousers, stretched them full length and handing them to the minister, asked him to point out the stains. Mr. Young said he had not examined the garment since it dried. He carefully looked at it and said the stains didn't seem as plain now as when the cloth was damp. Pointing to a discoloration near the knee he said: "I think those must be the stains we noticed."

Mr. Deering wanted to know if the pastor could positively swear that there were blood stains on the trousers. Witness replied that he could not. He was also unable to swear who owned the trousers or by whom they had been worn. He signed the complaint after the trousers were unearthed. Asked if he had made a chemical analysis of the stains, the minister replied:

"I have not; that isn't my business."

"Did you consider it your business to drive to East Baldwin and dig up old trousers?" Mr. Deering asked.

"I did, sir," was the reply.

Mrs. Walter Webb and her cousin, Mrs. Myrtle Files, who were also present when the trousers were unearthed, were briefly questioned. Mrs. Webb lived in the other part of the house occupied by Miss Broad, the murdered woman.

Sheriff Fogg and Deputy Sheriff Miles testified in regard to their part in the investigation of Lane. Deputy Miles, who has had a prominent part in hunting up evidence in the case, from the very first, admitted, under cross-examination, that in November Deputy Miles testified about his fruitless search for Miss Broad's pocketbook, which the Noble boy had found and thrown away again, while trapping on Cold Spring brook. In November, the deputy said, in answer to the county attorney's question, that he obtained from Lawyer Clifford, counsel for Walter Webb of Cornish, the first information about the finding of the pocketbook.

At this point, the state rested and the defense was begun. Leander C. Rounds of East Baldwin testified that the morning of August 20 he saw Lane ride on his bicycle in the direction of Gorham. This was between 8:30 and 9:30.

Lane, the respondent, was given a close examination. His testimony was, in substance, as follows:

He is 22 years of age, a native of Buxton, and has been lately employed as a farm hand in Standish. Last August, at the time of the Cornish fair, he and his wife were keeping house in what is known as Smut street, East Baldwin. On the evening of August 19, the first day of the fair, he had trouble with his father in law, George Sanborn, and they fought.

A warrant being sworn out by the grandfather, Lane borrowed his brother's bicycle the next morning and rode off to avoid arrest. He went to Buxton, called at the home of his father, William H. Lane, in Groveville, 20 miles from Cornish, took dinner there, then rode to Gorham, where his father had a crew of carpenters putting in a steel ceiling into the Orthodox church.

Lane talked with his father and workmen in the early part of the afternoon, then rode to South Gorham, two miles and called on a former neighbor, Freedom Moulton, arriving there about 3 o'clock and remaining three-quarters of an hour. Then he rode back to Gorham village, preceded his father to Groveville, got supper at his old home and then rode 20 miles to his own home in East Baldwin.

The next morning, he started for Cornish village in quest of a new house to hire, he thinking he could avoid arrest on the assault warrant by taking up a residence in another town. He tried to hire the abandoned house near where the body was found.

A suspicious circumstance connected with Lane's movements was that the night of the discovery of the murder he sold out his household goods to a neighbor at a great sacrifice, took his wife and brother, and started on the railroad track for Brownfield to Conway Center, Snow village and to Freedom, N. H, but he explains this by saying that he feared arrest.

Lane testified that he never knew Miss Broad or anything about her financial affairs. Cross examined by County Attorney Emery, the respondent admitted that at the time of his arrest, a week ago, he remarked to the detective: "You want me in that Cornish murder case, don't you?" He explained that he looked out of the window when the detective entered the house, and seeing a Cornish deputy sheriff took it for granted that the murder case, in regard to which he had been interviewed by several officers last fall, was what they were trying to connect him with. The respondent denied that he burned a hat or buried any trousers.

Then followed a long string of witnesses put on to establish an alibi for the respondent. They included Mrs. Ethel Lane, who saw him at Buxton the day of the murder, William H. Lane, the father whom he called upon at Gorham, Luther Lane, his brother, who also saw him at Gorham, Freedom Moulton of South Gorham upon whom he called, William Parker of Buxton whose house, Lane rode up to on a bicycle, Ernest Parker, who passed him at Groveville, Everett P. Elwell, who saw Arthur Lane call at the Gorham church, and others.

Mrs. Emma Sanborn, the respondent's mother in law, seemed to enjoy the humor of the occasion. She frequently interrupted her statements with outbursts of laughter. She denied that she had ever made incriminating statements about Arthur. The defending attorneys drew from her an admission that two weeks ago, shortly before Lane's arrest, that Mrs. Walter Webb of Cornish, one of the state's witnesses, gave her a hat and dress and the children some clothing.

The testimony was completed at 5:30. Tomorrow morning, the closing arguments will be made by County Attorney Emery and Mr. Deering. The defending attorneys predict the discharge of the respondent, and their prediction seems to be endorsed by most of the people of Cornish who have attended the hearing.

— **Portland Daily Press, June 3, 1903**

Arthur Lane Discharged

Cornish, June 3. - Arthur S. Lane, arrested in connection with the murder of Miss Olive Broad, was discharged by Trial Justice Randall today.

Justice Randall said he had thoroughly considered the evidence and before the arguments were made had decided in his own mind as to the weight of evidence.

— Portland Daily Press, June 4, 1903

Standish Man Shot By An Alleged Yegg

Battle in the Woods Near Sebago Lake
Gang of Five Overpowered -- Taken To Village
Wounded Man's Lung Penetrated But He May Recover

Alexander Rosborough, driver of a logging team, lies at the home of Marshall R. Higgins near Sebago Lake with a bullet wound in his right lung received late yesterday afternoon while helping run down five yeggmen who are suspected of having robbed the post office and two stores at West Buxton. The desperadoes, who were pursued for four miles in the woods between the Chadbourne neighborhood in Standish and the village of North Windham, were finally cornered by four citizens of Sebago lake and surrendered, being brought to the county jail last night by Sheriff Lewis W. Moulton and Deputy Sheriff Eugene Harmon.

Rosborough was shot by a man giving his name as Fred R. Dixon of Canada, Dixon and John T. Ryan, who claims to belong in Berlin N.H., being the only members of the gang who were armed. Dixon fired three times with a double action revolver, the first shot apparently being intended for Asa Douglass a clerk in the Sebago Lake Post Office and the General Store conducted by Postmaster Lemuel Rich. When Rosborough, whose only weapon was a "peavy" or lumberman's cant dog, which he took from his team, tried to head off the quintet of yeggs, Dixon fired at him twice, one bullet going through his coat and the other hitting him in the right breast.

The wounded man was taken to the Doctor William S. Thompson of Standish. He probed for the bullet for some time but was unable to find it, and last night he and Dr. Leonard O. Buzzell of Standish and Dr. Parker of Windham worked over Rosborough locating the bullet in the vicinity of the shoulder blade.

NOT CRITICAL

While Rosborough's condition is not considered critical, yet it is serious enough to warrant taking him to a hospital and he will be brought to this city sometime today. The physicians said last night that they believed he will recover unless he took cold and pneumonia developed. In that case, his chance of getting well would be rather slim.

The capture of the five men was one of the most sensational occurrences in Standish in a good many years, and on all sides the four boys who rounded them up are being complimented for the pluck that they showed in setting out after them and sticking right to the chase until they had got them. Lemuel Rich, the Postmaster, Asa Douglass, his clerk, Harry Paine, and Walter Libby, a rural mail carrier from the Sebago Lake office, were the men who took their lives in their hands and affected the capture of the alleged burglars, and although they knew that they were in all probability going up against a gang of desperate men who wouldn't hesitate to use gun play if they got within range, they didn't falter for an instant after hearing where the suspects were staying.

HAVE BEEN WATCHING

Ever since the robberies at West Buxton, suspicious characters have been seen in the vicinity of Sebago Lake and Standish villages and the people have been on the lookout. Tuesday, George Thompson of Standish, son of Granville Thompson, was driving in the direction of Sebago Lake when he gave some strangers who are supposed to have been a part of the quintet a ride. At that time, they had a grip but this seems to have disappeared, although Deputy Sheriff Harmon before leaving Sebago Lake last night directed that a search be instituted for it. It is possible that the money taken from the West Buxton post office may be in the grip, for the yeggs had very little about them when they were searched at the jail.

SANBORN MET MEN

Albert Sanborn of Sebago Lake also met the men for whom everybody was watching but when he saw them they didn't have any grip. It was generally believed that they were hanging around the community waiting for an opportunity to make a break at either the post office at Sebago Lake or that at Standish village but their hiding place could not be located. Yesterday afternoon, however, a brother of Rosborough, the man who was shot, furnished the first clue to their whereabouts. He saw tracks leading through the snow to the summer camp of R. H. Soule of South Windham, which is located near the shore of the lake and instantly reached the conclusion that the men were staying there. He at once notified Libby, the mail carrier, who in turn brought the matter to the attention of Postmaster Rich.

CITIZENS ARMED

Within a very short time Rich, Douglass, Libby, and Paine had armed themselves, Libby taking a Winchester rifle and the others Revolvers and, taking a couple of teams, they started for the camp. When they had driven within a short distance of the place, the yeggmen saw them coming and opening the door of their camp they beat a hasty retreat taking to a logging road that ran through the woods. The little posse of citizens urged their horses to a faster pace and the men ahead of them quickened their steps, but they didn't travel so fast as would have expected under the circumstances, apparently being tired.

FOUR MILE CHASE

They managed, though, to give their pursuers a drive of four miles before they were overtaken. Rosborough was coming along the logging road as the man hunt was in progress. He jumped from his team and taking his peavy joined Postmaster Rich's crew. After a while, the yeggs suddenly left the road and started into the woods, and then the other people were obliged to abandon their teams in order to keep up the pursuit. The chase continued for more than a quarter of a mile into the forest before the capture was made.

DIXON PULLED HIS GUN

Dixon pulled his gun when he and his companions saw that the other men were gaining on them and the first shot is believed to have been meant for Douglass. It went wide of the mark. Rosborough, the teamster, in his effort to head off the gang, flourished his peavy and in less time that it takes to tell it, he got his, the first bullet passing through his coat and the second striking him in the breast. Dixon, afterwards, said he didn't intend to shoot Rosborough but that his gun went off accidentally. The fact that he had previously fired one, though, and that he pulled the trigger twice the next time would not seem to substantiate this statement. He claims that when he saw the teamster coming with such a formidable looking weapon he thought it was about time to give up and so he had pulled out his revolver for the purpose of handing it over when the blamed thing went off, placing him in a very embarrassing position.

When the five were practically cornered and the only thing

left for them to do was to fight it out, they gave up, the sight of Libby's Winchester probably having considerable to do with influencing them to surrender.

"We's lost, and you fellows have won," one of them called out as they put up their hands, while Dixon and Ryan handed over their guns. The others were searched, but no weapons were found on them and then they were taken back to the village on a horse sled. Postmaster Rich and his men had nothing to bind them with, but having got their revolvers and being armed themselves they did not fear that they would make an attempt to escape.

HAD POSTAGE STAMPS

During the chase through the woods one of the yeggs threw away a box containing a lot of postage stamps and this was afterwards found in the snow by a man named Bonnett.

The news of the capture quickly spread throughout the town of Standish and other nearby communities and Sheriff Moulton was first notified by Albert H. Butterfield, the town clerk and treasurer and proprietor of a general store at Standish Village. The sheriff got the message about five o'clock and if he and Deputy Sheriff Harmon didn't do some hustling then nobody ever did. As soon as they could get ready, they started for the Union station to catch the train over the mountain division of the Maine Central railroad.

On the way to the station they fell in with somebody who had an automobile and jumping into this they managed to just reach the train before it pulled out. And they went to Sebago Lake, got the prisoners, and came back on the train that reaches Portland at eight o'clock. Isn't that going some? As soon as they reached the lake, Sheriff Moulton telephoned to the United States Marshal's office and he also notified the morning papers of the capture.

TOWN EXCITED

The yeggs were in the railroad station at Sebago Lake when the Sheriff and Deputy Harmon got there, and the waiting room was packed with people while a big crowd numbering little less than 200 people was gathering outside. A good many of the folks were armed, too, 'tis said for they didn't intend to take the slightest chance of the strangers getting away. Sheriff Moulton and Deputy Harmon, after notifying various people of the round-up, including Sheriff Charles O. Emery of York county, and looking about a little and hearing the story of the four men who effected the capture, were ready to return to the city. They handcuffed the yeggs securely and when they put them aboard the train, the crowd at the lake station began to melt away.

News that the men had been taken was spread all over this city within a very short time after it reached the sheriff's office, and so when the train from up country pulled in, there was a big crowd at the Union Station.

United States Deputy Marshall Burton M. Smith and Post Office inspector Spofford were among those to arrive and Deputy Sheriff Harry B. Hartford, whose home is in Standish was also there. The prisoners were hustled into a couple of hacks and it wasn't long before they were landed in jail.

THE NAMES GIVEN

There they gave their names as follows: Harry C. Morgan of Wales, John T. Ryan of Berlin N.H., Fred R. Dixon of Canada, and George Sullivan of New York. All of them appeared to be between the ages of 30 and 40, and Ryan was the heaviest one of the lot. On the whole, they were tough looking customers. It is understood that they made statements which lead the officers to believe they are the ones who broke into the West Buxton post office and the box of stamps that was found would be pretty good evidence, even if they had said nothing. After they had emptied their pockets and had been stripped, two pairs of shoes were found to have rubber on them. Rubber and other articles were taken from the store of Warren A. McCorrison at West Buxton.

PLAYED THE GAME

It is said that on the way to Portland one of the men said that they had played the game to the limit and lost. On Dixon, when his pockets were turned inside out, was a money bag that has been identified as one used by postmasters for keeping their change. He claimed when it was found on him that he had had it for seven years.

Deputy United States Marshal Smith came to the jail with the other officers and he took the men's names. He will probably investigate the case more fully today, and the men will be arraigned in the United States court for breaking and entering the post office.

Of course, everybody was delighted that the quintet had been captured and the four men who did the trick are having all sorts of nice things said about them for their exhibition of pluck. There was a rumor last night that Libby was so incensed when Rosborough was shot that he wanted to open fire on the desperadoes with his rifle, but he didn't have to, for they came down from their perch right away.

THE BUXTON ROBBERY

When the West Buxton post office was entered and the safe blown, from $50 to $100 worth of stamps and cash were taken, and at the McCorrison store, new rubbers were taken and the old ones left in the street. The other place visited was the dry goods store of John Berryman, a traveling man in the employ of the Clark-Eddy Co. of this city and there the cash drawer was rifled. The morning after the breaks, Oscar D. Rand, who lives about a mile and a half from West Buxton on the Bar Mills road, found that his horse was missing, and later in the day, the team was found standing in the road about four miles above West Buxton on the road leading to Sebago Lake. When questioned about the team last night, the five men who were taken into custody strenuously denied having taken it.

Some suspects were searched at Sebago Lake the day following the burglaries but they were allowed to go up the line on the 9:20 train. Later, the York county officials were not satisfied and so an officer went up the line and searched them again at North Conway. Nothing could be found on them though, and so, once more they were released. They had been employed cutting ice at the lake.

— **Portland Evening Express & Advertiser, January 29, 1912**

A Letter from Asa Douglass
to His Aunt Nellie Douglass Files

Dear Aunt Nellie,

Just got your letter, yes I had a pretty close call. I don't care to try it again. We got those fellows about 3 1/2 miles from here toward No. Gorham in the woods beyond Chadbourne's. Uncle Lewis will know pretty near. Chase them down a logging road for about (from our house up to Crockett's). When we came up to them in a place where they had dragged out logs, there Libby and I waited for them. Lem was right. Me and the fellow that done the shooting was ahead. He passed Lem and Libby and I took him and he had his hands in his pockets and stop him and asked him to take his hand out of his pockets. When he did, he made a grab for my gun with his right and stepped back just a little and fired at me but I threw back my head and the bullet did not hit me - when he fired Rosborough jumped and grabbed him and in the scrap he fired twice again - one going through Ross- right lung. Harry Paine and I both jumped for his gun but Paine was ahead of me. Lem and Libby had the other four in a line where they had drag out log. Libby saw the big fellow's gun sticking out of his pocket so he put the muzzle of his rifle right in his face, the fellow kinder warded it off and when he did, Libby reach over and took his gun. This happened before the shooter. If it hadn't possibly some of us would have got hurt because this would have given the rest of them courage.

The next day we found a gun where we took them so they had three and we think two more. They had plenty of cartridges. The choppers that are working for Mr. Roberts found two bags of money, a box of stamps, and stamp boxes, and a watch, and the gun.

They are starting a paper for the fellow that got hurt so to pay his expense in the hospital. There is a standing reward for of $200 a head that means if we get it $200 apiece, hope we do, especially Rosborough. This is a standard reward from the Government. The Press had the right account of it and you watch the Press they sent out for our pictures. I have not got any, only some Eva has taken.

Well, it is most mail time and I shall have to get busy as Lem has gone to Portland. Come up when you can. Give Eva's and my love to all the folk. — **Asa**
This is written in a hurry.

Asa Martin Douglass at this time was living in Sebago Lake Village, third house on the right from the intersection on what is now called Chadbourne Rd. At the time of this event, his wife, Geneva Libby Douglass was eight months pregnant with their first child, Lloyd - my father.

Mill Accident

Samuel Small, an employee of the Androscoggin Pulp Company had the two middle fingers on his right hand cut off up to the first joint while at work on the pressure pump. He is getting along as well as expected .

— Portland Daily Press, February 10, 1909

Pulp Mill - Steep Falls

Wild Cat Attack

A wild cat came to a window at Eleazer Parker's House, which lighted a room wherein three of his daughters were in bed, and leaping against the window sash which Eleazer heard, and thinking it was a cat that formerly been a domestic of the family, called to one of his daughters to open the window to the cat, to prevent her from breaking the glass; but scarcely had he spoken, when the cat, redoubling her strength, burst through a pane of glass into the room, and, from the table, leaped upon the bed, and seized the eldest girl by the nose, who cried to her father that the cat would kill her. He instantly sprung out of bed; ran into the room and caught the animal by one of her hind legs and drew her for the girl and bed, but in his effort the cat biting him thro' the arm, he was obliged to break his hold, and opening a door let in his dog, who began to run upon the cat but she resisted such violence that it compelled the dog to retreat; by which time he had lighted a candle, and immediately the cat grew timid and sought to hide under the bed clothes and soon fell easy prey to Eleazer.

About three weeks after this, the girl bitten was taken ill, and a physician being sent for, on presenting a cup of water to her, immediately discovered her disease, Hydrophobia (Rabies), to be occasioned by the bite of the cat - six days after which she died; and later her father, feeling uncommonly disordered, sent for his family physician, who declared him in the same condition that his daughter was in.

(Unknown newspaper obituary, February 24, 1812)

Depredations on the Town Magazine

March 29, 1831, By vote of the town in town meeting on the 29th day of March AD 1829 - The Treasurer was directed to call upon the persons who had committed depredations upon the town magazine to restore the property taken and if such persons neglected to restore the same by the first day of May, then next following to proceed according to law to obtain the same with damages - In attending to the duties above, assigned the following facts were ascertained - The lock by which the door of the magazine was supposed to be secured had for considerable time prior to the 1st of March 1830 been in such a situation that it was easily removed from the door without the aid of a key - The magazine had for several years been under the care of Thomas Shaw for which he had been paid by the selectmen or town - When the magazine was last inspected, there were 350 pounds of Balls 400 hand - red flints - There was found in the magazine by the selectman after the depredations 173 pounds of balls & 302 flints showing a deficiency of 177 pounds of balls & 98 flints - The persons against whom proof can be obtained of their taking away a part of this property are - A son of Mr. Thomas Shaw about 18 years old - two boys of Mr. Simeon Eaton - two boys of Mr. Isaac Davis - two boys of Mr. Jesse Butterfield, two boys of Mr. William Butterfield, all of which I believe are under fourteen years of age - After obtaining all the proof that could be relied upon, your agent endeavored to effect a compromise with the parents of these boys and made an estimate of the value of the property missing & divided it into five equal parts & proposed to each individual to give a note for his proportion & then to lay the whole subject before the town for them to act upon as they might deem proper on condition that no one of these notes should be valid unless each & every other of the five persons before named should settle or pay his proportion - to this proposition four of the individuals being Mr. Shaw, Mr. Eaton & the two boys of Mr. Butterfield acceded - But Mr. Shaw, at a subsequent time, refused to give his note & informed me that he had a large account against the town that must come into settlement - Mr. Eaton, about this time, moved out of the place - Mr. Jesse Butterfield & Mr. Wm Butterfield gave, each, a note for five dollars which are now in the hands of the Treasurer. Thus the only alternative left your Treasurer was to proceed criminally against these boys or prosecute Mr. Shaw for the whole amount of loss to the town - it was thought very doubtful whether the Treasurer wants to be justified in the first course & he did not feel authorized to prosecute half a dozen boys under fourteen years of age for theft without special direction of the town - & in the other case he thought it prudent to wait for the results of the settlement of Mr.

Shaw's account with the town as this might be brought in to the same adjustment by the committee - The Treasurer therefore asks to be excused from further duties upon this subject -

— **Resp^y Submitted - Oliver Frost Treasurer**
Town of Standish official document

Over the Dam

Steep Falls - Arthur Warren was dumping rubbish from a wheelbarrow into the Saco River when he lost his footing. After falling into the river and being carried over the dam, he managed cling to a rock in the river until he had rested and then swam to shore. It is a rather treacherous place in the river just above the dam and several who saw him go in expected to see him crushed to pieces as he went over the dam. His injuries summed up only a few scratches.

— Portland Express-Advertiser, May 2, 1910

Two Fatally Injured When Freight Crashes Team

STEEP FALLS—Mrs. Robert Ridlon, 39, died Tuesday evening as a result of an accident at the Maine Central Crossing in this village late Tuesday and Mrs. Charles Sanborn, 57, who was with her, died this morning. The horse they were driving was killed, the wagon shattered into a total wreck, and the women, hurled 40 to 50 feet by the impact, escaped instant death only by a miracle. Mrs. Ridlon was unconscious from the time she landed in the door yard of Mrs. Minnie Ridlon on the northeast side of the track and she died shortly after 10 in the evening. Dr. George I. Geer medical examiner, pronounced the cause of death shock and internal hemorrhage with concussion of the brain. Her left leg was broken below the knee, scrapes cuts and abrasions were numerous all over her body, and it was impossible to accomplish anything for her relief.

Mrs. Sanborn suffered fractures of both legs at the ankle, there was a deep cut in one thigh and a score of cuts and bruises showed that she was injured fatally also. It was thought last night that she would not survive and she passed away at 3 o'clock. Dr. Lorenzo

Norton of Mattocks, who was called was in constant attendance on the two women, at the bedside of Mrs. Sanborn ever since the death of Mrs. Ridlon. Dr. Samuel G. Sawyer of Cornish was called to assist him also.The two women started to drive from their homes on the Portland road, so-called, to K. of P. Hall to attend a social and even though it is but a short distance, perhaps a third of a mile, decided to ride over. The horse was owned by Mr. Ridlon, was docile and fearless, being driven for several years by his wife. They drove over the crossing on the main highway which is on the route to Mattocks without noticing any signs of a train approaching, drove in rear of the passenger station to the road leading toward Limington and failed to stop when a warning whistle was blown as the train neared the first crossing. This is 300 yards or such a matter from the northern or upper crossing.

Three times the engineer, making his first trip over the line as a driver, it is said, blew the whistle, short shrill blasts, as he had noticed the wagon and women occupants.

He applied the brakes, but the heavy freight special scarcely was retarded in its speed and the rig was hit squarely, both horse and wagon being hurled and rolled off the rails, the wagon occupants tossed high in the air and to the northeast side of the iron.

No one other than the engine crew saw the accident at the instant it happened and the first person to reach the scene was Harry Ridlon, brother of the dead woman's husband. He ran to their aid and a score or more gathered in two or three minutes. Brakes were applied hard to the train which stopped after running more than its full length past the crossing.

There is a clear view up the track for a distance of about 250 or 300 yards where the track makes a sharp curve and even down the line toward Portland a straight stretch for two miles or more is in full view but at times, freight cars on the siding and the buildings at the station are obstructions and it was in this direction that the train came from at high speed. To see full well, the women must have had to turn and look over their shoulders when close to the iron as the highway and railroad do not form a right angle at the crossing.

The two women lived nearly opposite the village library, with but one house between the Sanborn and Ridlon residences. They had lived many years in the village within plain sight of the lower crossing and by daily association kept track of train schedules. This train was a special freight, following the noon passenger train that runs through the mountain. They had no intimation that there was any danger undoubtedly.

Mrs. Ridlon was Sarah Robinson of Gray, an adopted daughter, at the time of her marriage 16 or 17 years ago. She had two sisters and a brother and her mother was living the last time she heard from her relatives but her adoption in her infancy led to dissolution of the family as no definite knowledge is available as to their whereabouts.

She was a church member, belonged also to the Pythian Sisterhood, was active in various village entertainment and social affairs and was well liked by all who knew her.

Mrs. Sanborn lived in her girlhood in East Limington and in

Steep Falls since her first marriage, there being two daughters, Mrs. Emma Hunkins of that village and Mrs. William Clark of Portland. She was conscious ever since she was hurt and her injuries occasioned her most acute suffering.

Despite the traffic over this Highway, the main line through Gorham, Standish and Baldwin, thence on to summer resorts on the west side of Sebago Lake and in the mountains, accidents have been almost unknown at either of these crossings. This fatality was on the lesser traveled road as the railroad really divides the village which is divided again by the Saco River, Standish, and Limington town boundary at this point.

— **Portland Express-Advertiser, November 7, 1917**

A Curious Story

A young man about 17 years of age, Libby by name, attended meeting at York's Corner, Standish, last Sunday evening, as all young men in that neighborhood should. During the services he left the house to get a drink of water. As he left the church, two men approached him to inquire the way to Abraham Came's house, and offered to pay him liberally if he would go with them in a covered carriage and show them they were coming. They were coming "right back," and would bring him with them. Having in prospect a generous fee, he consented to show them the way. After entering the carriage, one of the men placed his hand over Libby's mouth to prevent any outcry, while the other ransacked his pocket, and took from him his wallet and a knife. The men were disguised as negroes, and threatened, if he resisted, to kill him. After taking all the young man had in his pockets, they drove to the edge of a thick forest in Waterborough, near Carle's Corner, where one of the men left to take care of the horse and carriage, while the other carried the young man quite a distance into the woods, and erected a shanty of boughs for the accommodation of his prisoner. The food of the young man was crust of bread and cold water. Monday afternoon, as the keeper returned with some water for his prisoner, the prisoner managed to "hit him a clip" in the head, which felled him, and after "putting his boots" into him several times, he escaped, and after wandering some time in the woods, he succeeded in finding his way out, and reached his home at York's Corner, late Monday night, pretty well exhausted by his treatment and his travels. The above is all the young man can tell about the matter.

The men returned the wallet to Libby, but not his knife.

— Portland Argus, November 13, 1857

Italian's Bail is Defaulted

Bondsmen of Carmillo Lozzi in Liquor Case Must Make Good Bonds of $700. Carmillo Lozzi, the Italian who was arrested at Steep Falls, Tuesday, on a charge of the illegal possession of liquor and whose case was continued this morning, failed to make his appearance in court and his bail of $700 was ordered defaulted. His bondsmen were Barbato Napolitano and Bartolomeo Erasmo. The officers seized several barrels of beer from Lozzi at the time of his arrest. It is alleged that Lozzi was selling beer to a gang of Italians working on the foundation of a paper mill at Steep Falls. Complaint was made by George Johnson of Standish who, after drinking beer which he purchased from Lozzi, was robbed of $100 in the camp

— **Portland Daily Press, November 17, 1905**

Acknowledgments

The Standish Historical Society members who facilitate and encourage my work. Lil Barcaski and the team at GWN Publishing who do such fine work. The Journalists who, across time, have faithfully reported these tragic stories.

All proceeds from the sale of this book go to the Standish Historical Society.

About the author
Bruce L. Douglass

Bruce Douglass is the President of the Standish Historical Society working with a group of volunteers who are passionate about the rich history of Standish Maine. He is a retired Chemistry and Earth & Space Sciences teacher, Girl's Track & Field and Girls Cross Country Coach at Ledyard High School in Ledyard, CT. He has been a genealogist for over 50 years. Growing up in Scarborough, Maine, he retired to Standish, paradise, on Sebago Lake

Bruce previously compiled his grandfather's Sebago Lake camp diary, his father and grandmother's correspondence during WWII, his father-in-law's WWII letters from Leyte in the Pacific, and his mother and her mother's cookbooks. This is Bruce's second published book. *On This Day in Standish Maine* was published in June of 2024. A compilation of interesting tidbits, plucked from the files of the Standish Historical Society, that happened on each day of the year in Standish, the book is packed with historical moments from the last 200+ years.

www.ingramcontent.com/pod-product-compliance
Lightning Source LLC
Chambersburg PA
CBHW062131020426
42335CB00013B/1183